SALAD
DRESSING 101

SALAD
DRESSING 101

• dressings for all occasions •

edited by NATHAN HYAM

whitecap

Whitecap Books is known for its expertise in
the cookbook market, and has produced
some of the most innovative and familiar
titles found in kitchens across North America.
Visit our website at www.whitecap.ca.

Edited by Lesley Cameron
Design by Setareh Ashrafologhalai and
    Jacqui Thomas
Illustrations by Jacqui Thomas
Photography by Michelle Mayne

Printed in China

Library and Archives Canada Cataloguing in
Publication

    Salad dressing 101 / edited by Nathan
Hyam. — Rev. and updated

Includes index.
ISBN 978-1-77050-012-9

    1. Salad dressing. I. Hyam, Nathan, 1951–
II. Title. III. Title: Salad dressing one hundred
one.

TX819.S27S24 2010   641.8'14
C2009-906416-2

The publisher acknowledges the financial
support of the Government of Canada
through the Canada Book Fund (CBF) and
the Province of British Columbia through
the Book Publishing Tax Credit.

10 11 12 13 14   5 4 3 2 1

IMPORTANT: Some of the recipes in this
book call for the use of raw eggs. Pregnant
women, the elderly, young children and anyone with a compromised immune system
are advised against the consumption of raw
eggs. You may wish to consider the use of
pasteurized eggs. Visit www.eggsafety.org
and www.eggs.ca for information on eggs
and food safety.

Contents nts Contents Contents Contents Contents Contents C

Introduction

Salads and Dressings

Eating fresh raw food is a culinary link to our distant ancestors. Historical records show that the Romans, Egyptians and Babylonians all enjoyed various types of salads with flavored dressings as a part of their diet thousands of years ago. Foraging for greens and edible plants is part of our cellular memory. The word *salad* conjures up images of health, new growth and pleasant weather. Perhaps this is why eating salads can make you feel so good. They are an edible symbol of nature, a hint of green pastures or a lush country garden right at your table, no matter where you live.

The incredible diversity of produce available today makes an entire new range of dishes possible. However, although the multiplicity of greens and vegetables used in a salad will give a solid foundation of taste to the dish, most people would agree that the key flavoring element is the dressing. A perfectly matched dressing can tie together all the individual elements of a salad to create a culinary symphony.

Matching Dressings to Ingredients

There are infinite ways to transform a bowl of greens just by choosing an appropriate dressing. A carefully chosen dressing can transform a simple salad into a special occasion dish.

The dressing can be a spectacular combination of zesty flavors and aromas but it is best to remember that it is really a seasoning meant to enhance the main ingredients. It should augment their flavors, not overpower them. The art of matching a dressing to a salad calls for some analysis of both the salad ingredients and the dressing.

- Translucent mixtures of oil and vinegar, with added taste elements such as herbs, are best when paired with leafy greens.
- Creamy dressings with their thicker texture are ideal with heavier ingredients like vegetables, pastas, grains or potatoes and meats.
- Vinaigrettes (from the French *vin aigre*—"sour wine") are very versatile and can be used to dress most types of salads.

A question to ask in helping you choose a dressing is: Are the flavors of the salad ingredients predominantly strong or mild? A subtly flavored green like butter lettuce will be overwhelmed by a pungent creamy caesar dressing.

Texture is another important consideration. A soft, delicate mache leaf will be squashed by a heavy mayonnaise-based dressing, but the same dressing could be an ideal complement to sliced vegetables or a sturdy lettuce like romaine.

When a salad is a part of a larger meal it is important to determine whether or not the dressing will harmonize with the other flavors in the meal. The herbs or spices used in the salad dressing could complement the other flavors or clash. A weighty entrée like beef stew calls for a light leafy green salad with a simple oil and lemon dressing. A dressing based on orange juice could harmonize well with a curry entrée but it would be redundant with an entrée of orange ginger chicken.

When to Add the Dressing

The dressing for most salads, in particular leafy greens, should be added as close to serving time as possible, or served separately so the diner can decide on the amount to be added.

It is essential to be aware of the consequences of adding dressing to a green salad too far in advance of it being served. Most dressings contain acids such as vinegar or lemon juice. This acid will cause the greens to wilt and get soggy as soon as the salad is tossed with the dressing. The salad will get soggier as the time increases before it is eaten. However, this rule has an exception. Salads without leafy greens, such as potato or pasta salad, actually improve in flavor when they are allowed to marinate in the dressing for an hour or longer.

Emulsions

The two most common types of dressings are vinaigrettes and creamy dressings. These are both examples of emulsified dressings. Emulsifying means combining two liquids that don't usually mix together easily. In a salad dressing the two liquids would normally be oil and vinegar. Acidic liquids like vinegar or lemon juice help the process a little by changing the pH of the mixture.

Starting with the vinegar in a bowl, the oil is added very slowly, usually drop by drop, while beating vigorously. This disperses and suspends small drops of the liquids throughout each other. It is essential for the oil to be added slowly or the two liquids will not combine.

The two liquids will remain combined for a short period of time but will soon separate. The harder the mixture is beaten or stirred, the longer it will take to separate. This is because the oil and vinegar are broken into smaller droplets. The smaller the droplets are, the stronger the emulsion is.

To change the temporary emulsion into a permanent emulsion a third ingredient must be added—an emulsifier. Egg yolks and mustard are examples of emulsifiers. They act to stabilize the two different liquids by forming a layer around each of the tiny droplets and holding them in suspension. Mayonnaise is an example of a permanent emulsion. The harder a mayonnaise is beaten to break up the droplets, the more stable it becomes.

It is important to note that emulsions form more easily at room temperature because cold oil is more difficult to break up into small droplets that will create a more stable emulsion.

Quality of Ingredients

Most salad dressings are not cooked, so their flavor depends directly on the quality of the ingredients used. Cold-pressed fresh oils and well-made vinegars or freshly squeezed citrus juice are essential in creating a dressing that will enliven a salad with layers of subtle flavor and aroma. A hint of rancidity will cut through all the taste elements of any dressing.

Oils

- *Olive oil* has long been the most commonly used salad oil. Its range of flavors makes it very diverse. Choosing an olive oil is a bit like choosing a wine—there are hundreds of flavor possibilities from dozens of countries. Mediterranean countries produce the best olive oils but there are scores of subtle taste variations among them, from full-bodied rich olive flavors to more mellow-flavored mild herb notes. *Extra virgin olive oil* is the most flavorful olive oil and comes from the first pressing of high-quality olives. *Virgin olive oil* comes from a second pressing of the olives and is slightly more acetic. *Pure olive oil* comes from a subsequent pressing or from lower-quality olives. It has the least flavor and is also the least expensive.
- *Corn oil, safflower oil* and *canola oil* all have a very mild taste and are a popular base in many dressings because of their relatively neutral flavor.
- *Soybean oil* has a strong flavor and is not usually appropriate in salad dressings unless it has been blended with another oil.
- *Peanut oil* has a distinctive flavor if it is cold pressed and is ideal for Asian dressings.
- *Grapeseed oil* is a very healthy oil that is now more readily available. It has a very subtle nutty flavor that works well in many dressings.
- *Walnut oil* has a very rich walnut flavor that goes well with most greens. It does not keep for very long and should be refrigerated in warm weather.
- *Light oil* usually refers to an oil that is very mild in flavor. Canola oil would be an example of a light oil.

Vinegar

- *White or distilled vinegar* is distilled from a number of different grains. It has a high acidity level and a sharp, slightly medicinal taste that is not usually appropriate for salad dressings.
- *Red wine vinegar* is made from numerous types of red wines and the flavor will vary depending on the variety of wine used as well as whether or not it has been wood aged. It usually has a sharp, full-bodied flavor and is an excellent choice for vinaigrettes.
- *White wine vinegar*, like red wine vinegar, is made from many varieties of wine and will have the distinctive flavor of the wine from which it is made. It has a slightly sweeter and cleaner taste than red wine vinegar and is ideal in a vinaigrette served with milder greens.
- *Balsamic vinegar* is special wine vinegar made from sweet red wine that has been aged for years in wooden barrels. It is reddish brown in color and has a mellow, slightly sweet flavor. There are many different levels of quality but the best balsamic vinegar comes from Modena in Italy.
- *Sherry vinegar* is made from sherry and consequently has a rich smooth sherry flavor with a slight tartness. Its mellow full-bodied flavor is a result of being aged in wood barrels. The best sherry vinegars come from Spain.

- *Cider vinegar* is made from apples. It has sharp edge to it and a slight sweet apple flavor.
- *Rice vinegar* is made from rice wine. It is usually low in acidity and the flavors will vary depending on its country of origin. Chinese rice vinegar has a tangy flavor and is available in white, red and black. Japanese rice vinegar has a smoother, mellow taste and is available both natural and seasoned.
- *Fruit or herb vinegars* are made by infusing fruit or herbs in wine vinegar. They are readily available at gourmet shops but are also easy to make at home.

Matching Greens and Dressings

These symbols will help you to decide which dressing is best suited to the salad ingredient that you are using. It is important to remember that these suggestions are merely a basic guideline and the final decision is best determined by personal preference.

1 DELICATE MILD-FLAVORED GREENS
Butter (Boston) lettuce, green leaf lettuce, red leaf lettuce, mache, fresh herbs

2 STURDY ROBUST-FLAVORED GREENS
Romaine lettuce, endive, spinach, watercress, radicchio, sliced vegetables

3 STARCHES
Potatoes, noodles, rice

Vinaigrettes Vinaigrettes Vinaigrettes Vinaigrettes Vi

Toasted Pecan & Stilton Salad with Citrus Champagne Vinaigrette

serves 4 ❧ JUDY WOOD FROM *DISHING*

1	head butter lettuce
4 cups (1 L)	mesclun greens, loosely packed
1	green onion, finely chopped
1	orange, peeled and separated into segments
½ cup (125 mL)	toasted pecans
½ cup (125 mL)	Citrus Champagne Vinaigrette (see facing page)
½ cup (125 mL)	crumbled Stilton cheese

Tear the butter lettuce into bite-sized pieces and combine with the mesclun greens in a salad bowl. Add the green onion, orange segments, pecans and the vinaigrette and toss lightly. Add the Stilton and toss lightly again before serving.

Citrus Champagne Vinaigrette

makes 1½ cups (375 mL)

1	orange, juice only
½	lemon, juice only
¼ cup (60 mL)	champagne vinegar
1 tsp (5 mL)	finely chopped shallots
1 tsp (5 mL)	Dijon mustard
½ cup (125 mL)	olive oil
to taste	salt and freshly ground black pepper

Combine the lemon juice, orange juice, vinegar, shallots and mustard in a bowl. Slowly whisk in the oil. Add the salt and pepper to taste.

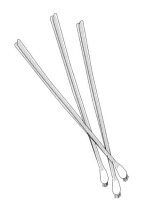

Basic Vinaigrette

makes about 1 cup (250 ml) 🌿 DANA McCAULEY FROM *PANTRY RAID*

3 Tbsp (45 mL)	white or red wine vinegar
1½ tsp (7.5 mL)	Dijon mustard
¾ tsp (4 mL)	each salt and pepper
pinch	granulated sugar
¾ cup (185 mL)	extra virgin olive oil

Stir vinegar, mustard, salt, pepper and sugar until mixed well. Whisking, drizzle in olive oil.

VARIATIONS   Tuscan Sunshine Substitute balsamic vinegar for wine vinegar and stir in 1½ tsp (7.5 mL) finely chopped fresh rosemary and 1½ tsp (7.5 mL) finely grated lemon peel.
Orchard Substitute cider vinegar for wine vinegar and stir in 1½ tsp (7.5 mL) chopped fresh thyme.
Red Peppercorn Crush ¾ tsp (4 mL) red peppercorns and add to vinegar mixture. Increase sugar to 1½ tsp (7.5 mL).
Saffron Soak ¾ tsp (4 mL) saffron threads in 1 Tbsp (15 mL) very hot water. Stir into vinegar mixture. Substitute vegetable oil for extra virgin olive oil.
Lemon Lime Substitute 1 Tbsp (15 mL) each lemon and lime juice for vinegar. Increase sugar to 1½ tsp (7.5 mL).

Tarragon Dressing

makes about ¾ cup (185 mL) ✤ JUDY WOOD FROM *DOUBLE DISHING*

¼ cup (60 mL)	red wine vinegar
1 Tbsp (15 mL)	sugar
1	clove garlic, minced
1 tsp (5 mL)	Dijon mustard
½ tsp (2 mL)	tarragon
½ cup (125 mL)	olive oil
to taste	salt and freshly ground black pepper

Combine the vinegar, sugar, garlic, mustard and tarragon in a bowl. Add the olive oil in a fine stream, whisking constantly. Season with salt and pepper.

Tarragon Vinaigrette

makes 1½ cups (375 mL)

MARY MACKAY FROM *GIRLS WHO DISH! SECONDS ANYONE?*

2 tsp (10 mL)	Dijon mustard
2 tsp (10 mL)	finely chopped shallots
1 tsp (5 mL)	sea salt
1 tsp (5 mL)	sugar
½ cup (125 mL)	raspberry vinegar
¾ cup (185 mL)	olive oil
3 Tbsp (45 mL)	chopped fresh tarragon
to taste	freshly cracked black pepper

In a small bowl, whisk together the Dijon mustard, shallots, salt, sugar and raspberry vinegar. Slowly whisk in the olive oil. Stir in the tarragon and black pepper.

Basil Balsamic Vinaigrette

makes ¾ cup (185 mL) ❧

ANNA AND MICHAEL OLSON FROM *INN ON THE TWENTY*

2 Tbsp (30 mL)	balsamic vinegar
6 Tbsp (90 mL)	extra virgin olive oil
¼ cup (60 mL)	fresh basil chiffonade
to taste	salt and pepper

Whisk ingredients together in a large bowl.

TIP Basil chiffonade is basil that is finely sliced. Stack the basil leaves on top of each other. Roll them up tightly into a cigar shape and then cut into very thin strips with a sharp knife.

Champagne Vinaigrette

makes ¾ cup (185 mL) JANET WEBB FROM *DOUBLE DISHING*

¼ cup (60 mL)	champagne vinegar
½ cup (125 mL)	olive oil
to taste	kosher salt and freshly ground black pepper

Whisk the vinegar into the oil, and season with salt and pepper.

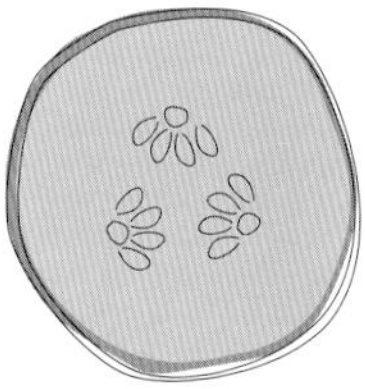

Citrus Vinaigrette

makes about 2 cups (500 mL) 🌿

OLAF MERTENS FROM *COOKING FROM THE HIP*

1 cup (250 mL)	orange juice
2	lemons, juice of
1½	limes, juice of
¼ cup (60 mL)	white wine vinegar
¼ cup (60 mL)	liquid honey
¼ cup (60 mL)	vegetable stock or water
¼ cup (60 mL)	vegetable oil
to taste	salt and white pepper

Place all the ingredients in a food processor or blender and mix for 2 minutes. Stop to adjust seasonings and blend for 30 seconds.

Keeps in the refrigerator for up to 7 days. Reblend or whisk before each use.

TIP If using bottled juices instead of real lemons or limes, check the bottle for equivalent measurements. Lemons and limes produce more juice and yield it more readily if they are at room temperature. If still cold, briefly microwave the fruit and roll on the counter with the palm of your hand before juicing. You will notice a big difference.

VINAIGRETTES

Citrus Vanilla Vinaigrette

makes about 1½ cups (375 mL) ✺

DEB CONNORS FROM *GIRLS WHO DISH! SECONDS ANYONE?*

1 cup (250 mL)	fresh orange juice
2 tsp (10 mL)	liquid honey
½	vanilla bean
2 Tbsp (30 mL)	rice wine vinegar
½ cup (125 mL)	canola oil
to taste	salt and freshly ground black pepper

Place the orange juice and honey in a small saucepan over high heat. Bring to a boil and reduce the heat to simmer.

Using a small sharp knife and a cutting board, cut the vanilla bean in half lengthwise. Holding the vanilla bean over the pot, use the knife to loosen some of the little black seeds from the bean into the orange juice. Place the pod in the juice and continue to simmer until the juice reduces to a glaze, about ¼ cup (60 mL).

When the juice is cool, remove the vanilla pod with your fingers, squeezing it to loosen more seeds. Using a small rubber spatula, scrape the contents of the saucepan into a blender. With the motor running, add the rice wine vinegar, then slowly add the canola oil. Season with salt and pepper and set aside.

Two-Citrus Vanilla Vinaigrette

makes about 1½ cups (375 mL) ✣ GAIL NORTON FROM *DISHING*

1 cup (250 mL)	olive oil
1	vanilla bean (with the seeds scraped out—use for another recipe), cut into 6 pieces
2	lemons, juice and zest of
2	oranges, juice and zest of
3 Tbsp (45 mL)	sherry vinegar
to taste	salt and freshly ground black pepper

In a large serving bowl, mix together the olive oil and vanilla bean. Slowly whisk in the juice and zest of the lemons and oranges, then the sherry vinegar. Season with salt and pepper.

Nice with roasted beets and fresh fennel.

Lemon Honey Dressing

makes 1½ cups (375 mL) 🌿

SUSAN MENDELSON AND JOEY CRUZ FROM *THE LAZY GOURMET*

1½ Tbsp (22.5 mL)	lemon zest
½ cup (125 mL)	lemon juice
½	clove garlic, sliced
1½-inch (4 cm)	piece ginger, sliced
1½ tsp (7.5 mL)	brown sugar
to taste	honey
6 Tbsp (90 mL)	canola oil
6 Tbsp (90 mL)	olive oil

In a saucepan, combine the lemon zest, lemon juice, garlic, ginger and brown sugar. Bring to a boil, then simmer over medium heat until the mixture is reduced by half.

Remove from the heat and mix in honey to the desired sweetness. Allow to cool to room temperature.

Purée the lemon mixture in a blender. Slowly add both oils while blending until the dressing has a creamy texture.

Spicy Orange Vinaigrette

makes about 1½ cups (375 mL)

SUSAN MENDELSON AND JOEY CRUZ FROM *THE LAZY GOURMET*

½ cup (125 mL)	orange juice
¼ cup (60 mL)	white wine vinegar
1	lime, juice of
2 Tbsp (30 mL)	chipotle chilies
2 Tbsp (30 mL)	chopped cilantro
1 tsp (5 mL)	ground cumin
¾ cup (185 mL)	canola oil
to taste	salt and freshly ground black pepper

Using a blender or food processor, blend together the orange juice, white wine vinegar, lime juice, chipotles, cilantro and cumin. With the blender running, slowly add in the oil until the dressing is creamy. Season with salt and pepper.

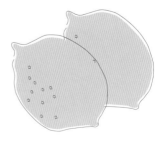

Tangerine Dressing

makes about ¾ cup (185 mL) ❧

DEE HOBSBAWN-SMITH FROM *DISHING*

½ tsp (2 mL)	ground star anise
1 tsp (5 mL)	grated fresh ginger
½ tsp (2 mL)	olive oil
2 tsp (10 mL)	maple syrup
2 tsp (10 mL)	finely grated tangerine zest
3–4 Tbsp (45–60 mL)	sunflower oil
⅓ cup (80 mL)	tangerine juice
3–4 Tbsp (45–60 mL)	lemon juice
to taste	salt and hot chili flakes

Combine the star anise, ginger, olive oil, maple syrup and zest in a small bowl. Add to a small pan and stir over high heat for 1 minute. Remove from heat and add the sunflower oil, citrus juices, salt and chili flakes. Mix well to combine.

Grapefruit Vinaigrette

makes ¾ cup (185 mL)

LESLEY STOWE FROM *GIRLS WHO DISH! SECONDS ANYONE?*

1 Tbsp (15 mL)	pink grapefruit juice
2	pink grapefruit segments (peeled)
1 tsp (5 mL)	finely chopped fresh ginger
1 tsp (5 mL)	finely chopped shallots
½	lime, juice of
¼ cup (60 mL)	extra virgin olive oil
to taste	salt and freshly ground black pepper

Purée the grapefruit juice, grapefruit segments, ginger, shallots and lime juice in a blender. With the motor running, add the olive oil in a steady stream until it is all incorporated. Season with salt and pepper.

VINAIGRETTES

Cranberry Tamari Dressing

makes about ¾ cup (185 mL) ❧ DANA McCAULEY FROM *PANTRY RAID*

1 cup (250 mL)	cranberry juice
2 Tbsp (30 mL)	tamari or soy sauce
2	cloves garlic, minced
1 tsp (5 mL)	Dijon mustard
½ tsp (2 mL)	each salt and pepper
2 Tbsp (30 mL)	extra virgin olive oil

Combine cranberry juice and tamari or soy sauce in a small saucepan. Bring to a boil and simmer rapidly for about 10 minutes or until reduced and syrupy. Remove from heat and stir in garlic, mustard, salt and pepper. Drizzle in oil while whisking constantly.

Raspberry Vinaigrette

makes about 1¼ cups (310 mL) ⚘ JOHN GARRETT FROM *HORIZONS*

⅓ cup (80 mL)	coarsely chopped raspberries, fresh or frozen
1 tsp (5 mL)	minced garlic
1 Tbsp (15 mL)	raspberry vinegar
½ cup (125 mL)	canola oil
3 Tbsp (45 mL)	extra virgin olive oil
1 tsp (5 mL)	sesame oil
2 Tbsp (30 mL)	chopped fresh parsley
to taste	sea salt and freshly ground black pepper

Combine all the ingredients in a small bowl.

TIP   Chop frozen berries quickly in a food processor while still frozen for a coarse, mealy texture.

Raspberry Poppyseed Dressing

makes about 1¼ cups (310 mL)

SUSAN MENDELSON AND JOEY CRUZ FROM *THE LAZY GOURMET*

½ cup (125 mL) mayonnaise
¼ cup (60 mL) raspberry vinegar
¼ cup (60 mL) sugar
¼ cup (60 mL) milk
2 Tbsp (30 mL) poppyseeds

Thoroughly mix all ingredients together with a whisk.

Sun-Dried Berry Vinaigrette

makes about 1½ cups (375 mL)

DAN ATKINSON FROM *SALMON HOUSE ON THE HILL COOKBOOK*

2 Tbsp (30 mL)	sun-dried cranberries
2 Tbsp (30 mL)	sun-dried blueberries
2 Tbsp (30 mL)	sun-dried raspberries
2 Tbsp (30 mL)	sun-dried cherries
⅓ cup (80 mL)	port
⅓ cup (80 mL)	water
2 tsp (10 mL)	liquid honey
pinch	salt and freshly cracked black pepper
1 tsp (5 mL)	lemon zest
1 tsp (5 mL)	lemon juice
2 tsp (10 mL)	balsamic vinegar
3 Tbsp (45 mL)	olive oil
1 tsp (5 mL)	chopped fresh basil
1 tsp (5 mL)	chopped fresh thyme
1 tsp (5 mL)	chopped fresh chives

Place the sun-dried fruits in a bowl. Pour the port and water over them and cover with plastic wrap. Place over a pot of simmering water for 30 minutes. Most of the liquid should be absorbed. Stir in the rest of the ingredients and refrigerate until needed.

Raspberry Rosemary Vinaigrette

makes about 1¼ cups (310 mL) ❧

DAN ATKINSON FROM *SALMON HOUSE ON THE HILL COOKBOOK*

¼ cup (60 mL)	raspberry vinegar
1 Tbsp (15 mL)	honey
2 tsp (10 mL)	minced onion
2 tsp (10 mL)	chopped fresh rosemary
2 tsp (10 mL)	chopped fresh chives
½ tsp (2 mL)	salt
1 tsp (5 mL)	black pepper
¼ cup (60 mL)	olive oil
½ cup (125 mL)	rosemary oil

Mix all the ingredients except the oils in a blender. Combine the oils and slowly add them while blending on medium speed. The vinaigrette can be refrigerated for up to 1 week.

Cranberry Pecan Dressing

makes about 1½ cups (375 mL) ❧ BILL JONES FROM *CHEF'S SALAD*

¼ cup (60 mL)   cranberry jelly (or sauce)
¼ cup (60 mL)   cranberry juice (or water)
2 Tbsp (30 mL)   mustard
½ cup (125 mL)   finely chopped toasted pecans
¼ cup (60 mL)   olive oil
to taste   salt and black pepper

Place the cranberry jelly, cranberry sauce, mustard and pecans in a mixing bowl. Drizzle in the olive oil, whisking constantly until smooth and thick. Season with salt and pepper.

Port Cherry Dressing

makes 1½ cups (375 mL) ❧ LESLEY STOWE FROM *INSPIRATIONS*

¼ cup (60 mL)	dried cherries
½ cup (125 mL)	late-bottled vintage port
1 tsp (5 mL)	grainy Dijon mustard
2 Tbsp (30 mL)	good-quality red wine vinegar
½ cup (125 mL)	extra virgin olive oil
to taste	sea salt and freshly ground black pepper

In a small saucepan over medium-high heat, simmer the cherries and port until the cherries are plump and approximately 1½ tsp (7.5 mL) of liquid remains. In a medium bowl combine the cherries and port with the mustard and vinegar. Gradually whisk in the olive oil. Season with salt and pepper.

Walnut Vinaigrette

makes 1½ cups (375 mL) 🌿 GAIL NORTON FROM *DOUBLE DISHING*

6 Tbsp (90 mL)	sherry vinegar
to taste	kosher salt
½ cup (125 mL)	walnut oil
3 Tbsp (45 mL)	olive oil
6 Tbsp (90 mL)	minced green onions
6 Tbsp (90 mL)	minced fresh parsley
3 Tbsp (45 mL)	finely minced shallots

Combine the sherry vinegar, salt, walnut oil and olive oil in a large mixing bowl. Whisk vigorously. Add the green onions, parsley and shallots and mix well.

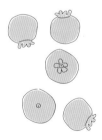

Honey Balsamic Vinaigrette

makes 2 cups (500 mL)

OLAF MERTENS FROM *COOKING FROM THE HIP*

⅓ cup (80 mL)	balsamic vinegar
1	lemon, juice of
4 tsp (20 mL)	Dijon mustard
3 Tbsp (45 mL)	liquid honey
3 Tbsp (45 mL)	finely chopped shallots or a small onion
½ tsp (2 mL)	fresh thyme
½ tsp (2 mL)	fresh oregano
1 cup (250 mL)	vegetable oil
to taste	salt and pepper

In a food processor or blender, mix all the ingredients, except the oil, salt and pepper. When completely smooth, and while still mixing, slowly drizzle in the oil. Stop and adjust seasonings. Blend for another 30 seconds. Keeps in the refrigerator for up to 7 days.

TIP   For a more refined dressing, let it sit for at least 24 hours to let the flavors really blend. Use a fine strainer to remove the little bits of herbs and onions. This will produce a velvety-smooth glaze for your salad.

Honey Caper Vinaigrette

makes ¾ cup (185 mL) ❦ ELLEN KELLY FROM *DISHING*

2	large cloves garlic
1 tsp (5 mL)	capers
½ tsp (2 mL)	salt
1 tsp (5 mL)	Dijon mustard
1 tsp (5 mL)	liquid honey
to taste	freshly ground black pepper
1 tsp (5 mL)	lemon juice
¼ cup (60 mL)	apple cider vinegar
½ cup (125 mL)	olive oil (or to taste)

Crush the garlic and capers with the salt. Add the mustard, honey, pepper, lemon juice and vinegar. Whisk in oil gradually until emulsified.

Quick Honey Mustard Dressing

makes about 2 cups (500 mL) 🌿 NATHAN HYAM

1 cup (250 mL)   liquid honey
¼ cup (60 mL)   lemon juice
2 Tbsp (30 mL)   Dijon mustard
½ cup (125 mL)   vegetable oil

In a large jar with a tight-fitting lid, combine the honey, lemon juice, mustard and vegetable oil. Cover and shake until thoroughly combined. Refrigerate until chilled and shake before serving.

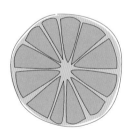

Pickled Ginger Vinaigrette

makes about 1¾ cups (435 mL) 🌿

SUSAN MENDELSON AND JOEY CRUZ FROM *THE LAZY GOURMET*

4 oz (125 g)	pickled ginger with juice
½-inch (1 cm)	piece baby ginger, peeled
3	cloves garlic
1	bunch cilantro
1	whole jalapeño pepper, stemmed
1 Tbsp (15 mL)	sambal badjak (see tip)
½ cup (125 mL)	rice wine vinegar
1 cup (250 mL)	light oil

Put all the ingredients in a blender and process on high until everything is well puréed. Will keep in the refrigerator for up to 2 weeks.

TIP   *Sambal badjak* is an Indonesian hot chili sauce. The best substitute is sambal oelek or an Asian-brand hot chili sauce.

2

Thai Dressing

makes 1 cup (250 mL) ❦ JANET WEBB FROM *DISHING*

2 Tbsp (30 mL)	hot chili oil
2 Tbsp (30 mL)	sesame oil
1	clove garlic, minced
⅓ cup (80 mL)	rice vinegar
3 Tbsp (45 mL)	tamari
¼ cup (60 mL)	olive oil
1	dried chili, crushed (optional)

Combine the chili oil, sesame oil, garlic, rice vinegar and tamari in a small bowl. Let stand for 30 minutes, then slowly whisk in the olive oil. Add the crushed chili, if using.

SALAD DRESSING 101

36

Lemon Ginger Vinaigrette

makes 1 cup (250 mL) ❦ BILL JONES FROM *CHEF'S SALAD*

2	lemons, juice and zest of
2 Tbsp (30 mL)	minced ginger
½ cup (125 mL)	light oil
to taste	salt and black pepper

Place the lemon juice, zest and ginger in a mixing bowl. Drizzle in the oil, whisking constantly, until smooth and thick. Season with salt and pepper.

VARIATION Substitute grapefruit, lime, orange or other citrus for the lemon.

VINAIGRETTES

Orange Ginger Sesame Dressing

makes about ¾ cup (185 mL) 🌿

DANA McCAULEY FROM *PANTRY RAID*

½ cup (125 mL)	orange juice
1 tsp (5 mL)	finely chopped crystallized ginger
1 Tbsp (15 mL)	rice wine vinegar
¼ tsp (1 mL)	salt
¼ tsp (1 mL)	cayenne pepper
1 Tbsp (15 mL)	toasted sesame oil
2 Tbsp (30 mL)	vegetable oil

Combine orange juice with ginger, rice wine vinegar, salt and cayenne. Whisk in the sesame and vegetable oils.

Thai Vinaigrette

makes about 1 cup (250 mL) 🌿

SUSAN MENDELSON AND JOEY CRUZ FROM *THE LAZY GOURMET*

3 Tbsp (45 mL)	lemon juice
2 Tbsp (30 mL)	brown sugar
1 Tbsp (15 mL)	fish sauce
½ tsp (2 mL)	Asian chili sauce
2 tsp (10 mL)	finely minced fresh ginger
¼ cup (60 mL)	minced green onion
¼ cup (60 mL)	minced fresh mint
2 Tbsp (30 mL)	minced basil
½ tsp (2 mL)	freshly grated nutmeg
¼ cup (60 mL)	canola oil

Combine the ingredients in a blender. Process on medium speed for 15 to 20 seconds, until puréed.

Cilantro Ginger Vinaigrette

makes about 1¾ cups (435 mL) ✤ JOHN GARRETT FROM *HORIZONS*

3 Tbsp (45 mL)	lime juice
1 Tbsp (15 mL)	rice vinegar
2 tsp (10 mL)	liquid honey
½ cup (125 mL)	chopped cilantro leaves
1 Tbsp (15 mL)	minced fresh ginger
1 Tbsp (15 mL)	sesame oil
¾ cup (185 mL)	olive oil
to taste	sea salt and freshly ground black pepper

In a small bowl, whisk all the ingredients together.
This can be made up to 2 hours in advance. Refrigerate
until needed.

Thai Mint Vinaigrette

makes about 1¾ cups (435 mL)

ANNE DONNELLY FROM *EAT TO THE BEAT* (EDITED BY LISA SLATER)

⅔ oz (20 g)	stalk lemongrass
3 Tbsp (45 mL)	fish sauce
1	lime, juice of
½ tsp (2 mL)	minced serrano chilies (with seeds)
½	bunch mint leaves
2	cloves garlic, peeled and chopped
1 cup (250 mL)	liquid honey
½ cup (125 mL)	vegetable oil

Remove outer leaves of lemongrass and place in food processor fitted with steel blade. Add fish sauce, lime juice, minced chili with seeds, mint, garlic and honey. Process until well blended. Gradually add oil and process until incorporated. Refrigerate until needed.

Asian Sesame Vinaigrette

makes ¾ cup (185 mL)

JENNIFER WARREN FROM *VEGETARIAN COMFORT FOOD*

1 Tbsp (15 mL)	sesame seeds
1 Tbsp (15 mL)	rice vinegar
1 Tbsp (15 mL)	soy sauce
2 tsp (10 mL)	Indonesian soy sauce (ketjap manis), or 1 tsp (5 mL) soy sauce and 1 tsp (5 mL) molasses
2 Tbsp (30 mL)	water
1	small clove garlic, chopped coarsely
1 Tbsp (15 mL)	sesame oil
¼ cup + 1 Tbsp (75 mL)	peanut oil

Preheat the oven to 375°F (190°C). Toast the sesame seeds on a small baking sheet in the oven for about 5 minutes, or until you can smell a rich sesame aroma. Let cool slightly.

Put all ingredients, including the sesame seeds, into a blender or food processor. Purée on high speed until the sesame seeds have broken into smaller pieces, 1 to 2 minutes.

Tapenade Vinaigrette

makes ¾ cup (185 mL) ☙

LESLEY STOWE FROM *GIRLS WHO DISH! SECONDS ANYONE?*

3 Tbsp (45 mL)	sherry vinegar
1	clove roasted garlic, mashed (see page 96)
1	clove garlic, crushed
2 tsp (10 mL)	black olive paste
½ cup (125 mL)	extra virgin olive oil
to taste	salt and freshly ground black pepper

Mix together the vinegar, both garlic cloves and olive
paste. Gradually whisk in the olive oil. Season with salt
and pepper.

Western ("French") Dressing

makes about 1¾ cups (435 mL) NATHAN HYAM

½ cup (125 mL)	ketchup
½ cup (125 mL)	canola oil
1 Tbsp (15 mL)	white wine vinegar
½ cup (125 mL)	sugar
¾ tsp (4 mL)	paprika
¼ tsp (1 mL)	dried mustard
¼ tsp (1 mL)	celery salt
¾ tsp (4 mL)	garlic salt

Place ketchup, oil and vinegar in a blender. Blend at high speed to combine well. While blending, gradually add sugar and spices. Blend thoroughly until everything is combined. Pour into a jar and refrigerate until needed.

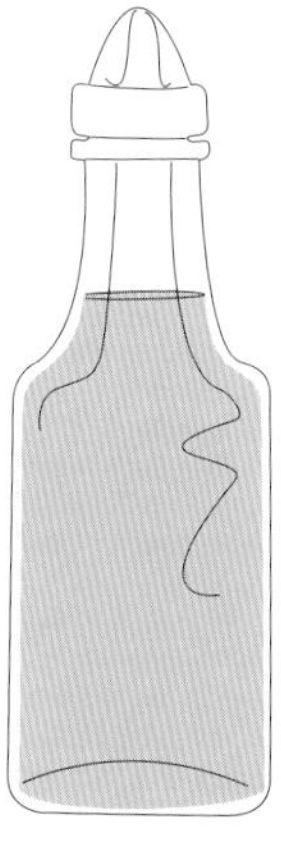

Anchovy Vinaigrette

makes about 1 cup (250 mL)

KAREN BARNABY FROM *GIRLS WHO DISH! SECONDS ANYONE?*

2 Tbsp (30 mL)	small drained capers
¼ cup (60 mL)	olive oil
2 Tbsp (30 mL)	lemon juice
1	clove garlic, minced
6	oil-packed anchovy fillets, finely chopped, not drained
2 Tbsp (30 mL)	finely diced onion
¼ cup (60 mL)	finely chopped fresh parsley

Finely chop half of the capers and set aside. Combine the olive oil, lemon juice and garlic. Add the anchovies, chopped and whole capers, onion and parsley. Stir well.

Fresh Tomato Dressing

makes 1 cup (250 mL)

NORENE GILLETZ FROM *THE FOOD PROCESSOR BIBLE*

1	clove garlic
2	ripe tomatoes, cut in chunks
¼ cup (60 mL)	fresh basil
2 Tbsp (30 mL)	olive oil (preferably extra virgin)
to taste	salt and freshly ground black pepper
pinch	sugar

Using a food processor fitted with a steel blade, drop the garlic through the feed tube while machine is running and process until minced. Add tomatoes and basil and process until finely chopped. Drizzle oil through the feed tube while machine is running; process until blended. Season with salt, pepper and sugar. Keeps for a day or two in the refrigerator.

SALAD DRESSING 101

Warm Mushroom & Sun-Dried Tomato Vinaigrette

makes about 3 cups (750 mL) 🌿

ANNA AND MICHAEL OLSON FROM *INN ON THE TWENTY*

6 Tbsp (90 mL)	olive oil, divided
2	shallots, minced
1 lb (500 g)	mixed mushrooms, including button, crimini, portobello, shiitake and oyster, cleaned and sliced
2	cloves garlic, minced
1 tsp (5 mL)	finely chopped fresh thyme
¼ cup (60 mL)	sun-dried tomatoes (reconstituted if not oil-packed), chopped
3 Tbsp (45 mL)	balsamic vinegar
to taste	salt and pepper
¼ cup (60 mL)	finely chopped green onions

Heat a large sauté pan over medium-high heat. Add 3 Tbsp (45 mL) of oil and the shallots and sauté for 1 minute. Add the mushrooms, garlic and thyme and sauté until mushrooms soften. Add sun-dried tomatoes and vinegar, and salt and pepper to taste. Cook for 2 minutes. Add the remaining olive oil and toss in green onions. Spoon immediately onto salad greens and serve.

Sun-Dried Tomato Vinaigrette

makes about 1½ cups (375 mL) ❧
MARY MACKAY FROM *INSPIRATIONS*

3 Tbsp (45 mL)	chopped sun-dried tomatoes
3 Tbsp (45 mL)	hot water
2 tsp (10 mL)	Dijon mustard
½ tsp (2 mL)	tomato paste
1	clove garlic
½ cup (125 mL)	chopped fresh basil leaves
1½ Tbsp (22.5 mL)	white wine vinegar
¼ cup (60 mL)	olive oil
6 Tbsp (90 mL)	tomato juice or water
to taste	fine sea salt and freshly ground black pepper

Soak the sun-dried tomatoes in the hot water for 5 minutes. Place the sun-dried tomatoes and soaking water, mustard, tomato paste, garlic clove, basil leaves and vinegar in a blender. Purée on high speed for about 15 seconds. Use a spatula to scrape down the sides of the blender.

Add the olive oil and blend until the dressing is smooth. Add the tomato juice or water, salt and pepper, and blend on high speed until smooth. The dressing should be slightly thickened, but thin enough to pass through a squirt bottle. Add more tomato juice or water if the dressing is too thick.

Transfer the dressing to a small squirt bottle, or place the dressing in a heavy plastic bag and make a small cut in the bottom corner when ready to squeeze out the dressing.

Red Onion Vinaigrette

makes about 1½ cups (375 mL) ❦ ELLEN KELLY FROM *DISHING*

¼ cup (60 mL)	finely diced red onion
2	cloves garlic, minced
½ cup (125 mL)	red wine vinegar
1 Tbsp (15 mL)	brown sugar
½ tsp (2 mL)	ground cumin
½ tsp (2 mL)	dried Mexican oregano
⅔ cup (160 mL)	good-quality olive oil
to taste	salt and freshly ground black pepper

Whisk all the ingredients together in a glass or ceramic dish with a lid.

Mustard Honey Pesto Vinaigrette

makes about 1½ cups (375 mL) ✹ CINDA CHAVICH FROM *DISHING*

1 Tbsp (15 mL)	fennel seeds
1 Tbsp (15 mL)	mustard seeds
3	dried red chili peppers, crushed
¾ tsp (4 mL)	salt
6 Tbsp (90 mL)	balsamic vinegar
3 Tbsp (45 mL)	Dijon mustard
3 Tbsp (45 mL)	pesto
1 Tbsp (15 mL)	liquid honey
¾ cup (185 mL)	extra virgin olive oil

Combine the fennel seeds, mustard seeds, chili peppers, salt, vinegar, mustard, pesto and honey in a food processor and process until the seeds are crushed. Add the olive oil and process to combine.

Mango Chutney Walnut Vinaigrette

makes about 1½ cups (375 mL) ✿ GAIL NORTON FROM *DISHING*

1	small onion, minced
3 Tbsp (45 mL)	olive oil
2 Tbsp (30 mL)	white wine vinegar
½ cup (125 mL)	minced fresh parsley
¼ cup (60 mL)	chopped cilantro
3 Tbsp (45 mL)	minced crystallized ginger
3 Tbsp (45 mL)	mango chutney
2 Tbsp (30 mL)	walnuts
to taste	salt and freshly ground black pepper

Briefly purée all the ingredients in a blender to combine. Wonderful with pasta or beans.

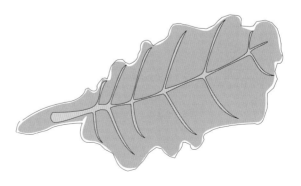

Italian Salad Dressing

makes about 1¼ cups (310 mL) ❧

NORENE GILLETZ FROM *THE FOOD PROCESSOR BIBLE*

1–2	cloves garlic
1 cup (250 mL)	olive or canola oil
¼ cup (60 mL)	red wine vinegar
1 Tbsp (15 mL)	lemon juice
½ tsp (2 mL)	dried mustard
¼ tsp (1 mL)	dried oregano
¼ tsp (1 mL)	sugar or honey
pinch	dried thyme and dried dill
1¼ tsp (6 mL)	salt (or to taste)
to taste	freshly ground black pepper

Using a food processor fitted with a steel blade, drop the garlic through the feed tube while machine is running and process until minced. Scrape down sides of bowl, add remaining ingredients and process until blended, about 5 seconds. Keeps about 1 month in a tightly closed jar in the refrigerator. Shake before using.

Sweet Vidalia Onion Dressing

makes 1½ cups (375 mL)

NORENE GILLETZ FROM *THE FOOD PROCESSOR BIBLE*

½	large Vidalia onion (about ½ lb/250 g)
¼ cup (60 mL)	canola oil
6 Tbsp (90 mL)	white vinegar
6 Tbsp (90 mL)	sugar (more to taste)
1½ tsp (7.5 mL)	dried mustard
¼ tsp (1 mL)	garlic powder
½ tsp (2 mL)	celery seed (or to taste)
½ tsp (2 mL)	salt
to taste	freshly ground black pepper

Cut off about ½ inch (1 cm) from one end of the onion and reserve. Pierce skin of remaining onion in several places with a sharp knife. Place cut side down in a microwavable bowl. Microwave on high for 3 to 4 minutes, until soft. Let cool and discard peel.

Peel the reserved onion and process with cooked onion in a food processor with steel blade until puréed, 10 to 12 seconds. You should have about ¾ cup (185 mL) purée. Add remaining ingredients and process a few seconds longer, until blended, scraping down sides of bowl as needed. Chill before serving. Refrigerate for up to 2 weeks.

Sweet & Spicy French Dressing

makes 1½ cups (375 mL) 🌿

NORENE GILLETZ FROM *THE FOOD PROCESSOR BIBLE*

1	clove garlic
¼ cup (60 mL)	ketchup
¼ cup (60 mL)	vinegar
¾ tsp (4 mL)	salt
¼ cup (60 mL)	sugar
¼ tsp (1 mL)	dried mustard
¼ tsp (1 mL)	paprika
¼ tsp (1 mL)	Worcestershire sauce
¾ cup (185 mL)	canola oil

Using a food processor fitted with a steel blade, drop the garlic through the feed tube while machine is running and process until minced. Scrape down sides of bowl. Add remaining ingredients and process until blended and creamy, 25 to 30 seconds. Keeps about 2 months in the refrigerator in a tightly closed jar.

Maple Syrup Vinaigrette

makes about 1¾ cups (435 mL)

JENNIFER WARREN FROM *VEGETARIAN COMFORT FOOD*

1 cup (250 mL)	olive oil
½ cup (125 mL)	balsamic vinegar
¼ cup (60 mL)	maple syrup
1 tsp (5 mL)	salt
½ tsp (2 mL)	pepper
1 tsp (5 mL)	dried basil leaves
4	small cloves garlic, crushed

Put all the ingredients into a jam jar, plastic container with a tight-fitting lid or blender/food processor. Shake or blend on low speed until the ingredients are combined.

Cal-Ital Dressing

makes ¾ cup (185 mL) 🌿 DANA McCAULEY FROM *PANTRY RAID*

2 Tbsp (30 mL)	balsamic vinegar
2 Tbsp (30 mL)	pesto
2	oil-packed sun-dried tomatoes, chopped
½ tsp (2 mL)	dried thyme leaves
¼ tsp (1 mL)	each salt and pepper
½ cup (125 mL)	extra virgin olive oil

Combine balsamic vinegar with pesto, sun-dried tomatoes, thyme, salt and pepper in a mini-chopper or blender. Chop well. Add olive oil and blend until well combined. Store tightly covered in the refrigerator for up to 1 week.

Walnut Dressing

makes about 1¼ cups (310 mL)

KATHLEEN SLOAN-McINTOSH FROM *A YEAR IN NIAGARA*

1 Tbsp (15 mL)	Dijon mustard
3 Tbsp (45 mL)	sherry vinegar
1 Tbsp (15 mL)	finely chopped fresh thyme
to taste	salt and freshly ground black pepper
¾ cup (185 mL)	olive oil
3 Tbsp (45 mL)	walnut oil

Whisk together the mustard, vinegar, thyme, salt and pepper. Slowly add the oils, continuing to whisk until slightly emulsified. Adjust the seasoning to taste.

Roasted Garlic Dressing

makes about 1 cup (250 mL)

SUSAN MENDELSON AND JOEY CRUZ FROM *THE LAZY GOURMET*

10	cloves garlic
	canola oil
¼ cup (60 mL)	balsamic vinegar
1 Tbsp (15 mL)	smooth Dijon mustard
¾ cup (185 mL)	olive oil

Preheat the oven to 350°F (175°C). Toss the garlic cloves in canola oil. Place in a piece of foil and seal. Roast in the oven for 20 to 25 minutes, or until the garlic has softened. Allow to cool.

In a bowl, combine the roasted garlic, balsamic vinegar and Dijon mustard. Mash until the garlic is puréed. Slowly whisk in the olive oil, until dressing is blended and smooth.

Southern Spiced Dressing

makes about 1 cup (250 mL) ❦ ERIC AKIS FROM *EVERYONE CAN COOK*

2	fresh or canned jalapeño peppers, finely chopped
⅔ cup (160 mL)	vegetable oil
4	limes, juice of
4 tsp (20 mL)	ground cumin
4 tsp (20 mL)	chili powder
4 tsp (20 mL)	sugar
to taste	salt and freshly cracked black pepper

Place the jalapeños, oil, lime juice, cumin, chili powder, sugar, salt and pepper in a bowl and whisk well.

VINAIGRETTES

Basic Coleslaw Dressing

makes 1½ cups (375 mL) ✻ NATHAN HYAM

2	cloves garlic, finely diced
2 Tbsp (30 mL)	finely diced onion
½ cup (125 mL)	lemon juice
1 Tbsp (15 mL)	Dijon mustard
1 tsp (5 mL)	crushed dried oregano
1 Tbsp (15 mL)	sugar
1 tsp (5 mL)	salt
½ tsp (2 mL)	black pepper
¾ cup (185 mL)	pure olive oil

Place all ingredients except oil in a bowl and stir together. Slowly whisk in the olive oil.

Creamy Dressings Creamy Dressings Creamy Dressi

Bitter Greens, Prosciutto & Apple with Camembert & Creamy Raspberry Vinaigrette

serves 4 ✎ JOHN GARRETT FROM *HORIZONS*

4 oz (125 g)	Camembert cheese (1 wheel)
1	Granny Smith apple
1⅓ cups (330 mL)	rinsed and roughly cut radicchio
1⅓ cups (330 mL)	Belgian endive sliced on the bias
1⅓ cups (330 mL)	mesclun greens
1	recipe Creamy Raspberry Vinaigrette (see facing page)
8	slices shaved prosciutto
to taste	freshly cracked black pepper

Divide the cheese into 12 wedges and distribute among 4 plates, placing the cheese toward the outside rim of the plates. Halve the apple and remove the core. Cut it into thin slices and fan a little sliced apple over each piece of cheese. Toss the radicchio, endive and mesclun greens with the raspberry vinaigrette. Divide evenly and place in the center of each plate. Loosely curl the prosciutto into small bunches and place 2 slices on top of each salad. Finish with cracked pepper over top.

Creamy Raspberry Vinaigrette

makes 1 cup (250 mL)

2	egg yolks
2 Tbsp (30 mL)	Dijon mustard
2 Tbsp (30 mL)	raspberry vinegar
1 tsp (5 mL)	fresh lemon juice
⅔ cup (160 mL)	canola oil
4	drops hot pepper sauce
½ tsp (2 mL)	sea salt

Place the egg yolks, mustard, vinegar and lemon juice in a small bowl and whisk. While whisking, slowly add the canola oil until incorporated. Season with hot pepper sauce and salt.

Mayo Magic
(Basic Safe Mayo)

makes 1¼ cups (310 mL) ❧ DANA McCAULEY FROM *PANTRY RAID*

¼ cup (60 mL)	pasteurized liquid eggs, well shaken
1 Tbsp (15 mL)	fresh lemon juice
2 tsp (10 mL)	Dijon mustard
pinch	each salt and white pepper
⅔ cup (160 mL)	vegetable oil

Combine eggs with lemon juice, mustard, salt and pepper in a blender. Mix until combined. Drizzle in oil with motor running. Blend until thick. Keeps in an airtight container in refrigerator for up to 2 weeks.

VARIATIONS   Roasted Garlic Add 1 Tbsp (15 mL) mashed roasted garlic before adding oil.
Indian Add ¾ tsp (4 mL) mild Indian curry paste and ¼ tsp (1 mL) finely grated lime peel before adding oil.
Basil Add 2 Tbsp (30 mL) chopped fresh basil before adding oil.

Creamy Herb Dressing

makes about 2¼ cups (560 mL)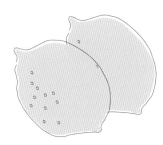

JOAN MONFAREDI FROM *EAT TO THE BEAT* (EDITED BY LISA SLATER)

2 cups (500 mL)	mayonnaise
¼ cup (60 mL)	fresh lemon juice
2 Tbsp (30 mL)	chopped fresh herbs (thyme, parsley, chives etc.)
to taste	salt and pepper

Place all the ingredients in a small bowl and whisk to combine.

Blue Cheese Dressing

makes 1½–2 cups (375–500 mL) ☙ NATHAN HYAM

½ cup (125 mL)	blue cheese
2 Tbsp (30 mL)	sherry vinegar
1	clove garlic, crushed
dash	Worcestershire sauce
¼ tsp (1 mL)	cracked black pepper
1–1½ cups (250–375 mL)	heavy or whipping cream (35%)

Place the blue cheese in a bowl and crumble into small pieces with a fork. Mix in the sherry vinegar, garlic, Worcestershire sauce and black pepper. Slowly stir in 1 cup (250 mL) of cream with a fork and keep stirring until the mixture is creamy but still lumpy. Allow the dressing to sit at room temperature to thicken for 5 minutes before using. If a thinner dressing is desired, stir in remaining ½ cup (125 mL) cream as required. Keep refrigerated and mix before using.

Gorgonzola Dressing

makes about 1¾ cups (435 mL)

KAREN BARNABY FROM *INSPIRATIONS*

4 oz (125 g)	Gorgonzola cheese, rind removed
1 cup (250 mL)	sour cream
¼ cup (60 mL)	mayonnaise
1 Tbsp (15 mL)	red wine vinegar
1 tsp (5 mL)	minced garlic
to taste	salt and freshly ground black pepper

Crumble the cheese and mash it to a paste. Slowly stir in the sour cream, then the mayonnaise, vinegar and garlic. Season with salt and pepper.

Creamy Gorgonzola Dressing

makes about 1¼ cups (310 mL) ❦ JOHN GARRETT FROM *HORIZONS*

6 oz (175 g)	Gorgonzola cheese, crumbled
⅓ cup (80 mL)	extra virgin olive oil
⅓ cup (80 mL)	canola oil
2 Tbsp (30 mL)	herb vinegar
2 tsp (10 mL)	balsamic vinegar
2 Tbsp (30 mL)	liquid honey
2 tsp (10 mL)	lemon juice
2 tsp (10 mL)	chopped fresh tarragon
2 tsp (10 mL)	chopped fresh mint
2 tsp (10 mL)	chopped fresh basil
½ tsp (2 mL)	minced fresh ginger
½ tsp (2 mL)	minced fresh garlic
½ tsp (2 mL)	grainy mustard
½ tsp (2 mL)	freshly ground black pepper
¼ tsp (1 mL)	sea salt

Place all the ingredients in a small bowl and whisk to combine. This vinaigrette will keep for up to 1 week in the refrigerator.

TIP Basil or tarragon vinegar would be a good choice for this dressing.

Stilton Buttermilk Dressing

makes 1½ cups (375 mL)

DAN ATKINSON FROM *SALMON HOUSE ON THE HILL*

6 oz (175 g)	Stilton cheese, grated
1 tsp (5 mL)	Dijon mustard
1 tsp (5 mL)	lemon juice
1 tsp (5 mL)	lemon zest
pinch	salt
1½ tsp (7.5 mL)	lemon pepper
1 cup (250 mL)	buttermilk

In a mixing bowl combine the cheese, mustard, lemon juice and zest, salt and lemon pepper. Whisk in the buttermilk.

This can be refrigerated for up to a week. Leftovers can be used as a vegetable dip or salad dressing.

Spinach & Sour Cream Dressing

makes about 1 cup (250 mL) ✥ BILL JONES FROM *CHEF'S SALAD*

2	lemons, juice and zest of
½ cup (125 mL)	sour cream
2 tsp (10 mL)	minced garlic
2 tsp (10 mL)	hot sauce
½ cup (125 mL)	blanched spinach (or frozen, thawed and drained)
to taste	salt and black pepper

Place the lemon juice and zest, sour cream, garlic and hot sauce in a blender. Process the mixture until smooth. Squeeze any excess water from the spinach and drop it into the blender. Pulse to a smooth green purée. Thin with a little water, if necessary, to make a pouring consistency. Season with salt and pepper.

VARIATION Substitute coconut milk for the sour cream and add 2 tsp (10 mL) curry paste.

Creamy Spinach
Salad Dressing

makes about 1½ cups (375 mL) ✴ NATHAN HYAM

1 cup (250 mL)	pure olive oil
5 Tbsp (75 mL)	red wine vinegar
¼ cup (60 mL)	sour cream
2 Tbsp (30 mL)	sugar
2 Tbsp (30 mL)	chopped fresh parsley
1½ tsp (7.5 mL)	salt
½ tsp (2 mL)	dried mustard
⅛ tsp (0.5 mL)	cracked black pepper

Place all ingredients in tightly sealed jar and shake until completely combined.

Creamy Dill Salad Dressing

makes about 1½ cups (375 mL)

NORENE GILLETZ FROM *THE FOOD PROCESSOR BIBLE*

2–4	cloves garlic (or ½ tsp/2 mL garlic powder)
¼ cup (60 mL)	fresh dill (or 1 tsp/5 mL dried dill)
1 cup (250 mL)	mayonnaise (light or regular)
6 Tbsp (90 mL)	vinegar
to taste	salt and freshly ground black pepper

Using a food processor fitted with a steel blade, drop the garlic and dill through the feed tube while machine is running. Process until minced. Add remaining ingredients and process until blended, about 5 seconds. Keeps about a week in the refrigerator.

VARIATION Use ½ cup (125 mL) mayonnaise and ½ cup (125 mL) sour cream.

Russian Salad Dressing

makes about 1⅓ cups (330 mL)

NORENE GILLETZ FROM *THE FOOD PROCESSOR BIBLE*

¼	small onion
1 cup (250 mL)	mayonnaise
2 Tbsp (30 mL)	chives or green onions
⅓ cup (80 mL)	chili sauce or ketchup

Using a food processor fitted with a steel blade, drop the onion through the feed tube while machine is running; process until minced. Add remaining ingredients and process until combined. Keeps about a week in a tightly covered container in the refrigerator.

VARIATION   Thousand Island Dressing Add 3 Tbsp (45 mL) relish or 2 small minced gherkins.

Creamy Garlic Dressing

makes about 1¼ cups (310 mL)

NORENE GILLETZ FROM *THE FOOD PROCESSOR BIBLE*

2	cloves garlic
2 Tbsp (30 mL)	fresh parsley (or 1 tsp/5 mL dried parsley)
1 cup (250 mL)	cottage cheese
¼ cup (60 mL)	buttermilk
2 Tbsp (30 mL)	white vinegar
pinch	dried tarragon
to taste	salt and freshly ground black pepper

Using a food processor fitted with a steel blade, drop the garlic and parsley through the feed tube and process until minced. Add remaining ingredients and process until smooth and creamy, about 30 seconds, scraping down bowl once or twice. Refrigerate until needed. Keeps 4 to 5 days in the refrigerator.

Marty's Garlic Cheese Dressing

makes about 1 cup (250 mL)

NORENE GILLETZ FROM *THE FOOD PROCESSOR BIBLE*

1–2	large cloves garlic
2 oz (60 g)	low-fat mozzarella or brick cheese
1–2 Tbsp (15–30 mL)	grated Parmesan cheese
¼ cup (60 mL)	red wine vinegar
½ cup (125 mL)	olive or canola oil
½ tsp (2 mL)	lemon juice
¼ tsp (1 mL)	Worcestershire sauce
¼ tsp (1 mL)	Italian seasoning
to taste	salt and freshly ground black pepper (or mixed peppercorns)

Using a food processor fitted with a steel blade, drop the garlic through the feed tube while machine is running. Process until minced. Cut mozzarella or brick cheese in 1-inch (2.5 cm) chunks. Process until finely chopped, 20 to 25 seconds. Add remaining ingredients and process until combined, about 15 seconds longer. Store in a jar in the refrigerator. Wait a few hours before serving to allow flavors to blend. Shake thoroughly before serving. If too thick, thin with a little water. Keeps about 2 weeks in the refrigerator.

CREAMY DRESSINGS

Creamy Dressing #1

makes about 1¼ cups (310 mL)

JENNIFER WARREN FROM *VEGETARIAN COMFORT FOOD*

1 cup (250 mL)	plain yogurt
1	very small clove garlic, coarsely chopped
2 Tbsp (30 mL)	olive oil
2 heaping Tbsp (35–40 mL)	chopped fresh parsley
½ tsp (2 mL)	salt

Put all the ingredients into a food processor and process until smooth, about 1 minute, scraping down the sides of the processor halfway through.

Creamy Dressing #2

makes about 1½ cups (375 mL)

JENNIFER WARREN FROM *VEGETARIAN COMFORT FOOD*

½ cup + 2 Tbsp (155 mL)	light mayonnaise
6 Tbsp (90 mL)	plain yogurt
6 Tbsp (90 mL)	water
8	miniature sweet pickled onions, coarsely chopped
2 tsp (10 mL)	chopped fresh parsley
2 tsp (10 mL)	liquid honey
2	large pinches mustard powder
½ tsp (2 mL)	salt

Put all the ingredients into a food processor and process until smooth, about 1 minute, scraping down the sides of the processor halfway through.

Green Goddess Salad Dressing

makes about 1½ cups (375 mL)

NORENE GILLETZ FROM *THE FOOD PROCESSOR BIBLE*

1–2	cloves garlic
4	green onions, cut in chunks
¼ cup (60 mL)	fresh parsley
1 can	anchovies, drained
½ cup (125 mL)	sour cream or yogurt (regular or low fat)
½ cup (125 mL)	mayonnaise (regular or low fat)
3 Tbsp (45 mL)	white wine vinegar
2–3 Tbsp (30–45 mL)	fresh lemon juice
to taste	freshly ground black pepper

Using a food processor fitted with a steel blade, drop the garlic through the feed tube while machine is running. Process until minced. Add green onions, parsley and anchovies. Process until minced. Add remaining ingredients and process until blended, scraping down sides of bowl once or twice. Refrigerate until needed. Keeps about 10 days in the refrigerator.

Avocado Green Goddess Dressing

makes 1¼ cups (310 mL) ❧ DANA McCAULEY FROM *PANTRY RAID*

1	ripe avocado, about 8 oz (250 g)
¾ cup (185 mL)	water
1 tsp (5 mL)	finely grated lime peel
3 Tbsp (45 mL)	lime juice
2	green onions, chopped
1	clove garlic
½ tsp (2 mL)	ground cumin
½ tsp (2 mL)	salt
¼ tsp (1 mL)	pepper

Halve the avocado. Peel, and remove stone. Chop flesh and place in a blender. Add water, lime peel, lime juice, green onions, garlic, cumin, salt and pepper. Blend until smooth. Taste and adjust seasoning if necessary. Keeps covered in the refrigerator for up to 3 days.

CREAMY DRESSINGS

Creamy Green
Curry Dressing

makes about 1½ cups (375 mL)

DANA McCAULEY FROM *PANTRY RAID*

½ cup (125 mL)	mayonnaise
½ cup (125 mL)	sour cream, yogurt or mayonnaise
4 tsp (20 mL)	Thai green curry paste
2	stalks celery, chopped
2	green apples, cored and chopped
¼ cup (60 mL)	chopped fresh parsley (optional)
to taste	salt

Stir mayonnaise with sour cream, yogurt or more
mayonnaise, curry paste, celery, apples and parsley
(if using) until evenly combined. Taste and season
with salt.

Creamy Indian
Curry Dressing

makes about 1 cup (250 mL) ❦ DANA McCAULEY FROM *PANTRY RAID*

⅔ cup (160 mL)	mayonnaise (light or regular)
1 Tbsp (15 mL)	mild Indian curry paste
2 tsp (10 mL)	white wine vinegar
2 tsp (10 mL)	minced fresh ginger
1 tsp (5 mL)	grated lime peel
2 tsp (10 mL)	lime juice
to taste	salt and pepper

Stir mayonnaise with curry paste, vinegar, ginger, lime peel and lime juice in a large bowl. Taste and add salt and pepper as necessary.

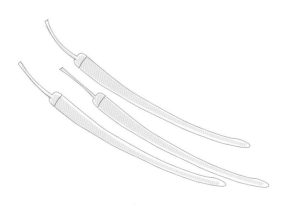

Mango Chutney Cream

makes about 1¼ cups (310 mL)

DANA McCAULEY FROM *PANTRY RAID*

1 cup (250 mL)	mayonnaise (light or regular)
1 Tbsp (15 mL)	mild Indian curry paste
1 Tbsp (15 mL)	mango chutney
to taste	salt and pepper

Stir mayonnaise with curry paste and chutney. Add salt and pepper to taste.

Orange Peanut Ginger Dressing

makes about 1 cup (250 mL) ❦ DANA McCAULEY FROM *PANTRY RAID*

⅓ cup (80 mL)   orange juice
¼ cup (60 mL)   peanut butter
1 Tbsp (15 mL)   soy sauce
1 Tbsp (15 mL)   hoisin sauce
½ tsp (2 mL)   minced fresh ginger
1   small clove garlic, minced
¼ cup (60 mL)   lightly packed cilantro leaves

Stir orange juice, peanut butter, soy sauce, hoisin sauce, ginger and garlic until smooth. Stir in cilantro leaves.

CREAMY DRESSINGS

Pickled Ginger & Avocado Dressing

makes about 1 cup (250 mL) ❧ BILL JONES FROM *CHEF'S SALAD*

¼ cup (60 mL)	pickled ginger
2 Tbsp (30 mL)	light soy sauce
2 tsp (10 mL)	sesame oil
¼ cup (60 mL)	water
2	avocados, peeled, seeded and chopped
2	limes, juice and zest of
to taste	salt and black pepper

Place the pickled ginger, soy sauce, sesame oil, water, avocado, lime juice and zest in a blender. Process until smooth and season well with salt and pepper. Thin with a little water, if necessary, to make a pouring consistency. Chill until needed.

Thai Peanut Mango Dressing

makes about 2½ cups (625 mL)

ANNE DONNELY FROM *EAT TO THE BEAT* (EDITED BY LISA SLATER)

1 lb (500 g)	green mango, peeled
4 oz (125 g)	red and green peppers, sliced into thin strips
½ tsp (2 mL)	salt
1½	limes, juice of
3 Tbsp (45 mL)	vegetable oil
2 Tbsp (30 mL)	garlic, chopped
1 bunch	green onions, sliced
3 Tbsp (45 mL)	fish sauce
3 Tbsp (45 mL)	crunchy peanut butter
3 Tbsp (45 mL)	brown sugar
¼ tsp (1 mL)	ground black pepper
¼ cup (60 mL)	seeded and finely chopped serrano chilies
¼	red onion

Cut mango into julienne strips and place in a large bowl. Add thin strips of green and red peppers. Sprinkle with salt and lime juice.

Heat vegetable oil in a medium frying pan. Add garlic and green onions. Cook until garlic is softened. Lower heat and add fish sauce, peanut butter, brown sugar, pepper and chili pepper. Cook until peanut butter has melted. Stir well and remove from heat.

Pour over mango and peppers in bowl. Add red onion and mix thoroughly. Chill completely before using.

CREAMY DRESSINGS

Thai Coconut Caramelized Garlic Dressing

makes about 1¾ cups (435 mL) 🌿

NATHAN HYAM FROM *NEW THAI CUISINE*

1 cup (250 mL)	coconut milk
¼ cup (60 mL)	crispy fried shallots
¼ cup (60 mL)	crispy fried garlic
1 tsp (5 mL)	hot sauce
1 Tbsp (15 mL)	palm or brown sugar
½	lime, juice of
¼ cup (60 mL)	cilantro leaves

Combine the coconut milk, shallots, garlic, hot sauce, sugar and lime juice in a saucepan. Bring to a boil. Add the cilantro. Purée the mixture in a blender.

VARIATION   One cup (250 mL) chicken stock can be used instead of coconut milk for a lower-fat version of this dressing.

Thousand Island Dressing

makes about 2 cups (500 mL) ✎ NATHAN HYAM

1 cup (250 mL)	mayonnaise
¼ cup (60 mL)	ketchup
2 Tbsp (30 mL)	white vinegar
4 tsp (20 mL)	sugar
4 tsp (20 mL)	sweet pickle relish
2 tsp (10 mL)	finely minced white onion
¼ tsp (1 mL)	salt
dash	black pepper

Combine all of the ingredients in a small bowl. Stir well. Place in a covered container and refrigerate for a few hours, stirring occasionally, so that the sugar dissolves and the flavors blend.

Horizons Caesar Salad

serves 4 ❧ JOHN GARRETT FROM *HORIZONS*

1	egg yolk
2 tsp (10 mL)	Dijon mustard
1 Tbsp (15 mL)	chopped garlic
4 tsp (20 mL)	red wine vinegar
1 Tbsp (15 mL)	lemon juice
2 tsp (10 mL)	minced capers
2	anchovy fillets, minced
½ cup (125 mL)	extra virgin olive oil
½ cup (125 mL)	canola oil
1 tsp (5 mL)	Worcestershire sauce
dash	hot pepper sauce
to taste	sea salt and freshly ground black pepper
8	herb focaccia sticks, about 4 inches long (10 cm) each
1	large head romaine lettuce
1 cup (250 mL)	grated Parmesan cheese

You can either whisk the dressing together by hand or use a food processor. If you are making it by hand, put the egg yolk, mustard, garlic, vinegar, lemon juice, capers and anchovies in a mixing bowl, then whisk to combine. Combine both oils in a liquid measuring cup and slowly pour them into the egg mixture while whisking. The key to success here is to pour the oil in a very fine stream until the mixture starts to thicken. When about half the oil is incorporated, you can begin to pour it in a little faster.

Whisk in the Worcestershire and hot pepper sauce and season with salt and pepper. If you feel the dressing is too thick, whisk in a little more vinegar. If it seems too thin, add more oil. If you are using a food processor, simply put all the ingredients except the oils into the food processor bowl. With the motor running, slowly add all the oil.

To make the crostini, you can use any kind of bread you like and cut it any way you like. This recipe uses herb focaccia bread, cut into strips. Place bread on a baking sheet, drizzle with a little extra virgin olive oil and season with salt and pepper. Bake at 350°F (175°C) for 5 to 10 minutes, or until golden brown and crisp.

Cut the lettuce into bite-sized pieces. Plunge the pieces into ice-cold water and let soak for 5 minutes. Remove and shake off the excess water or spin in a salad spinner. (If the lettuce is too wet, it will dilute the dressing.)

In a large bowl, toss the lettuce with the dressing and half the Parmesan cheese. Set out 4 plates and crisscross 2 focaccia crostinis on each plate. Distribute the salad evenly among the plates. Sprinkle the remaining cheese on top.

Safe Caesar Dressing

makes about 1 cup (250 mL) ❦ DANA McCAULEY FROM *PANTRY RAID*

¼ cup (60 mL)	pasteurized liquid eggs, well shaken
2 Tbsp (30 mL)	grated Parmesan cheese
2 Tbsp (30 mL)	red wine vinegar
1 Tbsp (15 mL)	lemon juice
1 tsp (5 mL)	Dijon mustard
½ tsp (2 mL)	Worcestershire sauce
½ tsp (2 mL)	anchovy paste
¼ tsp (1 mL)	pepper
2	small cloves garlic
¾ cup (185 mL)	extra virgin olive oil
to taste	salt

Combine the eggs with the Parmesan, vinegar, lemon juice, mustard, Worcestershire sauce, anchovy paste, pepper and garlic in a blender. Blend until well mixed. With motor running, drizzle in olive oil. Taste and add salt to taste. Use immediately or cover and store in refrigerator for up to 7 days.

TIP   Because this recipe uses pasteurized liquid eggs, you won't have to worry about the health issues associated with classic caesar recipes.

Classic Caesar Dressing

makes about 1¼ cups (310 mL) 🌿

CAREN McSHERRY FROM *MORE THAN SALT AND PEPPER*

4	cloves garlic, chopped
2 tsp (10 mL)	Worcestershire sauce
1	small lemon, juice of
2 Tbsp (30 mL)	Dijon mustard
2	egg yolks
12	anchovy fillets
2 tsp (10 mL)	freshly ground tellicherry or black pepper
1 cup (250 mL)	extra virgin olive oil

Place the garlic, Worcestershire sauce, lemon juice, mustard, egg yolks, anchovies and pepper in the bowl of a food processor fitted with a steel blade. Pulse a few times, stopping to scrape down the sides of the bowl. With the machine running, slowly pour in the olive oil in a thin, steady stream, until the dressing emulsifies and becomes smooth and creamy. Taste, adjust the seasonings and chill until ready to serve.

Caesar Vinaigrette

makes about 1½ cups (375 mL)

OLAF MERTENS FROM *COOKING FROM THE HIP*

3	cloves garlic, roasted (see below)
3 Tbsp (45 mL)	white wine vinegar
2 Tbsp (30 mL)	lemon juice
1 Tbsp (15 mL)	Dijon mustard
1 Tbsp (15 mL)	anchovy fillets, drained
1 Tbsp (15 mL)	capers, drained
¼ tsp (1 mL)	Worcestershire sauce
⅛ tsp (0.5 mL)	hot pepper sauce
1 cup (250 mL)	vegetable or olive oil
to taste	salt and white pepper

In a food processor or blender, or with a hand whisk, mix together all the ingredients except the oil, salt and pepper. Blend to make a smooth mixture. While still mixing, drizzle in the oil very slowly. When all the oil has been added, stop to taste. Season and blend one more time.

Keeps in refrigerator for up to 7 days. Reblend or whisk before each use.

TIP Roast the garlic for this recipe to maximize flavor. Take a whole garlic bulb, place on a piece of foil, sprinkle with some olive oil and tightly wrap in the foil. Bake at 350°F (175°C) for 20 minutes. Carefully open the foil, remove the bulb and squeeze out the creamy garlic from each clove. Alternately, take about a third of the oil from the recipe and roast the peeled garlic cloves in it until lightly browned.

Modern Caesar Dressing

makes about 1¼ cups (310 mL)

SUSAN MENDELSON AND JOEY CRUZ FROM *THE LAZY GOURMET*

1	egg
2 Tbsp (30 mL)	capers
4	cloves garlic
1 Tbsp (15 mL)	Dijon mustard
¼ cup (60 mL)	red wine vinegar
¾ cup (185 mL)	olive oil
to taste	salt and freshly ground black pepper

Place the egg in boiling water for 90 seconds. Remove and set aside. In a food processor or blender, blend the capers, garlic, Dijon mustard, red wine vinegar and the coddled egg. With the machine running, slowly pour in the olive oil, until the mixture becomes thick and creamy. Season with salt and pepper.

Creamy Caesar Dressing

makes about 1½ cups (375 mL) ❧ KAREN MILLER FROM *DISHING*

16	cloves garlic, roasted in skin (see page 96)
2	lemons, juice of
2 tsp (10 mL)	Dijon mustard
2 tsp (10 mL)	sea salt
2 Tbsp (30 mL)	cracked black pepper
2 tsp (10 mL)	granulated sugar
1 cup (250 mL)	olive oil
2–4 Tbsp (30–60 mL)	whipping cream

Whisk together the garlic, lemon juice, mustard, salt, pepper and sugar. Slowly add the olive oil in a stream until it has emulsified, then add cream to taste. Adjust seasonings if necessary.

Caesar Dressing

makes about 1½ cups (375 mL)

NORENE GILLETZ FROM *THE FOOD PROCESSOR BIBLE*

1–2	cloves garlic
¾ cup (185 mL)	canola or olive oil
¼ cup (60 mL)	wine vinegar
1 Tbsp (15 mL)	lemon juice
1 tsp (5 mL)	Worcestershire sauce
½ tsp (2 mL)	sugar
½ tsp (2 mL)	salt
to taste	freshly ground black pepper
¼–⅓ cup (60–80 mL)	Parmesan cheese

Using a food processor fitted with a steel blade, drop the garlic through the feed tube while machine is running. Process until minced. Add oil, vinegar, lemon juice, Worcestershire sauce, sugar, salt, pepper and Parmesan cheese. Process 8 to 10 seconds to blend. Refrigerate until needed.

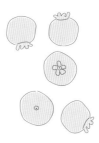

Light & Delicious Caesar Dressing

makes about 1¼ cups (310 mL)

ERIC AKIS FROM *EVERYONE CAN COOK*

6	cloves garlic, crushed
1 Tbsp (15 mL)	Dijon mustard
1 tsp (5 mL)	sugar
⅔ cup (160 mL)	2% yogurt
2 tsp (10 mL)	anchovy paste (optional)
1 Tbsp (15 mL)	red wine vinegar
¼ cup (60 mL)	lemon juice
1 Tbsp (15 mL)	Worcestershire sauce
1 tsp (5 mL)	hot pepper sauce
to taste	salt and freshly cracked black pepper

Place the garlic, mustard, sugar, yogurt, anchovy paste (if using), vinegar, lemon juice, Worcestershire sauce, hot pepper sauce, salt and pepper in a large bowl and whisk well to combine.

Minted Caesar Dressing

makes about 1½ cups (375 mL)

SHELLEY ROBINSON FROM *DOUBLE DISHING*

2	cloves garlic
1	anchovy fillet
2 tsp (10 mL)	Dijon mustard
1	medium egg
1	lemon, juice and zest of
¼ cup (60 mL)	fresh mint leaves
2 tsp (10 mL)	sugar
1 cup (250 mL)	olive oil
to taste	salt and freshly ground black pepper

Place the garlic, anchovy, mustard, egg, lemon juice and zest, mint leaves and sugar in a food processor or blender, and process to combine. With the machine running, slowly drizzle in the 1 cup (250 mL) olive oil. Season to taste with salt and pepper. Refrigerate until ready to use.

Salmon House Caesar Dressing

makes about 3 cups (750 mL)

DAN ATKINSON FROM *SALMON HOUSE ON THE HILL COOKBOOK*

1	egg
2 Tbsp (30 mL)	grated Parmesan cheese
1 Tbsp (15 mL)	minced garlic
4	anchovy fillets in oil
1 tsp (5 mL)	salt
½ tsp (2 mL)	freshly ground black pepper
1½ Tbsp (22.5 mL)	capers and juice, puréed
1½ Tbsp (22.5 mL)	Dijon mustard
3 Tbsp (45 mL)	sour cream
dash	hot pepper sauce
1 tsp (5 mL)	Worcestershire sauce
1 tsp (5 mL)	soy sauce
1½ cups (375 mL)	vegetable oil
¾ cup (185 mL)	olive oil
1½ Tbsp (22.5 mL)	lemon juice
1½ Tbsp (22.5 mL)	red wine vinegar

Place the egg, Parmesan cheese, garlic, anchovies and oil, salt, pepper, capers and juice, mustard, sour cream, hot pepper sauce, Worcestershire sauce and soy sauce in a mixing bowl and stir together. Mix the oils together. Combine the lemon juice and vinegar. Add the oil and the vinegar mixture alternately until the dressing is thick.

Thai Creamy Caesar Dressing

makes about 2 cups (500 mL) ✌ NATHAN HYAM

3	cloves garlic, peeled and diced
½ strip	anchovy fillet, chopped
1 tsp (5 mL)	red curry paste
½ cup (125 mL)	chopped fresh parsley
¼ cup (60 mL)	chopped fresh cilantro
1 Tbsp (15 mL)	lime juice
½ tsp (2 mL)	Worcestershire sauce
¼ tsp (1 mL)	salt
¼ tsp (1 mL)	black pepper
1 cup (250 mL)	mayonnaise
1 Tbsp (15 mL)	Dijon mustard
¼ cup (60 mL)	cold water

Place garlic, anchovy, red curry paste, parsley, cilantro, lime juice, Worcestershire sauce, salt and pepper into the food processor and purée till everything is a paste.

Measure the mayonnaise into a bowl and whisk the Dijon mustard into the mayo. Whisk the puréed garlic-parsley mixture into the mayonnaise. Then whisk in the water until the desired texture is achieved. Keeps in the refrigerator for about a week.

New Wave Chicken with White Zinfandel Vinaigrette

serves 4 as a main course or 8 as a side dish ✣

DEE HOBSBAWN-SMITH FROM *SKINNY FEASTS*

4	chicken breasts, skinned and boned
2	Granny Smith apples, sliced
2	stalks celery, sliced
1 bunch	green onions, chopped
¼ cup (60 mL)	minced fresh thyme
½ cup (125 mL)	dried zucchini
½ cup (125 mL)	Caramelized Pecans (see facing page)
4 cups (1 L)	mixed greens
1 cup (250 mL)	White Zinfandel Vinaigrette (see page 108)

Pan-steam the chicken breasts until cooked, about 5 to 7 minutes. Slice or shred the cooled chicken into bite-sized pieces. Toss in a large bowl with the remaining ingredients except for the greens and half of the dressing. Toss the greens separately with the reserved vinaigrette, arrange on individual plates and top with the chicken mixture.

Caramelized Pecans

makes about 4 cups (1 L)

4 cups (1 L)	pecan halves
4 cups (1 L)	boiling water
2 Tbsp (30 mL)	unsalted butter
¼ cup (60 mL)	sugar
½ tsp (2 mL)	salt
1 tsp (5 mL)	cayenne
1 tsp (5 mL)	ground star anise

Place the nuts in a colander or strainer and, holding them carefully over the sink, pour the boiling water over them. The water helps minimize the tannins in the skins without making the nuts soggy.

Combine the nuts and remaining ingredients in a nonstick sauté pan. Cook over medium-high heat until the pecans are dark and glossy, about 5 to 10 minutes. Shake and stir constantly to prevent burning. Once the nuts are crisp and brown, spread them in a thin layer on a baking sheet lined with parchment. Let them cool entirely. Store, wrapped well, in freezer.

(continued on next page)

(continued from previous page)

White Zinfandel Vinaigrette

makes 1½ cups (375 mL)

1 bottle (750 mL)	white Zinfandel
¼–½ cup (60–125 mL)	honey
1	lime, zest of
¼ cup (60 mL)	lime juice
2 Tbsp (30 mL)	Dijon mustard
to taste	salt and hot chili flakes
½ cup (125 mL)	canola oil
2 Tbsp (30 mL)	minced fresh thyme

In a nonreactive pot, reduce the wine to about ½ cup (125 mL). Transfer it to a bowl and mix with the honey, lime zest and juice, mustard and the salt and chili flakes. Whisk in the oil slowly, mixing continuously to form an emulsion. Stir in the fresh thyme.

VARIATION Ginger Zin Vin Add 2 Tbsp (30 mL) puréed fresh ginger or finely slivered pickled ginger.

Light of Heart
Tarragon Dressing

makes about 1½ cups (375 mL)

OLAF MERTENS FROM *COOKING FROM THE HIP*

1 cup (250 mL)	water
½	lemon, juice of
2 Tbsp (30 mL)	tarragon vinegar
2 Tbsp (30 mL)	white wine vinegar
½ tsp (2 mL)	Dijon mustard
2 Tbsp (30 mL)	sugar
½ cup (125 mL)	vegetable oil
¼ cup (60 mL)	olive oil
to taste	salt and white pepper

Place all the ingredients in a blender or food processor and mix well. This keeps in the refrigerator for up to 7 days. Reblend or whisk before each use.

Roasted Pepper Lime Vinaigrette with Lovage & Miso

makes about 1 cup (250 mL) 🌿

DEE HOBSBAWN-SMITH FROM *SKINNY FEASTS*

1	roasted pepper, sweet or hot
3	cloves garlic
1 Tbsp (15 mL)	miso (see tip page 136)
2	limes, juice and zest of
½ cup (125 mL)	rice vinegar or sherry vinegar
3 Tbsp (45 mL)	honey
1 Tbsp (15 mL)	grainy mustard
⅓ cup (80 mL)	canola oil
2 Tbsp (30 mL)	lovage leaves
to taste	salt and hot chili flakes

Purée the pepper and garlic in a food processor, then add the miso, limes, vinegar, honey and mustard. Add the oil and lovage slowly, with the machine running. Balance the flavors with salt and hot chili flakes.

Roasted Pepper and Rosemary Vinaigrette Omit the miso and lovage, and add 1 Tbsp (15 mL) minced fresh rosemary and/or fresh thyme.

Roasted Pepper and Cilantro Vinaigrette Omit the lovage, and add 1 tsp (5 mL) roasted sesame oil and 1 Tbsp (15 mL) fresh cilantro.

Roasted Pepper and Olive or Caper Vinaigrette Omit the lovage and miso, and add 2 Tbsp (30 mL) chopped olives or capers, and 2 Tbsp (30 mL) minced fresh parsley or chives.

Roasted Pepper and Balsamic Vinaigrette Omit the lovage, limes and miso, add 1 Tbsp (15 mL) minced fresh rosemary and substitute 2 Tbsp (30 mL) balsamic vinegar for the sherry or rice vinegar.

Light Tarragon Vinaigrette

makes 1 cup (250 mL)

LIZ PEARSON AND MAIRLYN SMITH FROM *THE ULTIMATE HEALTHY EATING PLAN*

⅓ cup (80 mL)   extra virgin olive oil
⅓ cup (80 mL)   red wine vinegar
¼ cup (60 mL)   honey
2 tsp (10 mL)   dried basil
1 tsp (5 mL)   paprika
1 tsp (5 mL)   dried tarragon
1 tsp (5 mL)   freshly cracked pepper

Whisk together all the ingredients. Can be stored in the refrigerator for up to 1 week.

Prairie Sage Vinaigrette

makes about 1¼ cups (310 mL)

DEE HOBSBAWN-SMITH FROM *SKINNY FEASTS*

3 Tbsp (45 mL)	grainy mustard
¼ cup (60 mL)	honey
½ cup (125 mL)	sage-infused vinegar (see below)
¼ cup (60 mL)	minced fresh sage
2 Tbsp (30 mL)	minced fresh chives or green onions
½ cup (125 mL)	canola oil
to taste	salt and hot chili flakes

Combine all the ingredients except the oil, salt and chili flakes. Mix well, then slowly whisk in the oil to form an emulsion. Season to taste with salt and hot chili flakes.

TIP Herb-infused vinegars are a quick, easy way to add flavor to food. Start with good, flavorful vinegar, and pick or buy fresh herbs at the height of the season when they are cheap and plentiful. Stuff clean herbs and spices into jars, cover them with vinegar and steep for a month before using. Softer herbs like basil and sage need to be strained out and discarded after the steeping time has elapsed.

LOW-FAT RECIPES

Hazelnut Vinaigrette

makes about 1¼ cups (310 mL) ❦

DEE HOBSBAWN-SMITH FROM *SKINNY FEASTS*

¼ cup (60 mL)	hazelnuts, toasted, skinned and chopped
1 Tbsp (15 mL)	puréed fresh ginger
2 Tbsp (30 mL)	minced lemon thyme
1 Tbsp (15 mL)	smooth Dijon mustard
1	lime, juice and zest of
¼ cup (60 mL)	sherry vinegar
¼ cup (60 mL)	honey
⅓ cup (80 mL)	canola oil
to taste	salt and hot chili flakes

Whisk together all the ingredients. Store in the refrigerator until needed. If keeping this dressing more than 1 day, omit the chopped nuts and add them just before using the dressing to keep them from going soft.

VARIATION Pistachio Mint Vinaigrette Omit the hazelnuts and thyme, replacing them with equal amounts of undyed pistachios and fresh mint.

TIP Hazelnuts are one of the finest nuts in the world for cooking and eating but their skins defeat many people. To convince hazelnuts to shed their skins, spread them in a single layer on a baking sheet and pop into a medium-hot oven, about 375°F (190°C). Check them every 5 to 7 minutes, and when the skins slip off easily when rubbed between your fingers, it's time to remove them from the oven. Transfer the nuts to a kitchen towel and roll them up for 5 minutes. The steam generated will loosen any stubborn skins. Roll the nuts in the towel to remove the skins, popping any recalcitrant nuts that won't shed back into the oven for a second toasting.

Maple Thyme Vinaigrette

makes 1½ cups (375 mL)

DEE HOBSBAWN-SMITH FROM *SKINNY FEASTS*

⅓ cup (80 mL)	maple syrup, preferably dark
⅓ cup (80 mL)	thyme-infused white wine vinegar (see tip page 113)
2 tsp (10 mL)	Dijon mustard
1	lemon, juice and zest of
½ cup (125 mL)	canola oil
½ cup (125 mL)	minced fresh lemon thyme or thyme
to taste	salt and freshly ground black pepper

Whisk together all the ingredients. Taste and balance the flavors. Set aside until needed.

Triple Citrus Vinaigrette

makes about 1 cup (250 mL) 🌿

DEE HOBSBAWN-SMITH FROM *THE QUICK GOURMET*

1 Tbsp (15 mL)	smooth Dijon mustard
¾ cup (185 mL)	mix of lemon, lime and orange juice
to taste	salt and hot chili flakes
¼ cup (60 mL)	olive oil
1–2 Tbsp (15–30 mL)	melted honey
1 Tbsp (15 mL)	minced fresh thyme or chives
1 Tbsp (15 mL)	minced fresh chives

Whisk together the mustard, citrus juice, salt and hot chili flakes. Slowly add the oil, whisking to form an emulsion. Add the honey and herbs, using the larger amount of honey if needed to balance the flavors. Store in the refrigerator for up to a week.

VARIATIONS   Asian Vinaigrette Add 1 Tbsp (15 mL) soy sauce, ¼ cup (60 mL) chopped cilantro and 1 Tbsp (15 mL) sesame oil. Fruit Vinaigrette Stir in ½ cup (125 mL) finely minced or puréed mango, grated raw apple or cooked puréed apple.

Summer Peach Vinaigrette

makes ¾ cup (185 mL)

DEE HOBSBAWN-SMITH FROM *THE QUICK GOURMET*

1	ripe peach, peeled and minced
1	lime, juice and zest of
2 Tbsp (30 mL)	maple syrup
3 Tbsp (45 mL)	canola oil
to taste	salt and hot chili paste

Combine all the ingredients, mashing the peach bits into tiny pieces or not, as you like.

Caramelized Apple Vinaigrette

makes about 1 cup (250 mL)

DEE HOBSBAWN-SMITH FROM *SKINNY FEASTS*

1	organic apple
¼ cup (60 mL)	melted honey
¼ cup (60 mL)	apple cider vinegar
1 Tbsp (15 mL)	puréed fresh ginger
1 Tbsp (15 mL)	grainy Dijon mustard
2 Tbsp (30 mL)	fresh herbs—your choice of thyme, basil, marjoram, oregano, parsley, tarragon
2 Tbsp (30 mL)	canola oil
to taste	salt and hot chili flakes

Wash the apple well and do not peel it. Slice into about 8 pieces, removing the core. Cook the apple slices in a nonstick pan without any oil until they are well colored. Slice, chop or purée them in a food processor, then add the remaining ingredients to form an emulsified vinaigrette.

Balsamic Vinaigrette

makes about 1 cup (250 mL)

DEE HOBSBAWN-SMITH FROM *THE QUICK GOURMET*

1 Tbsp (15 mL)	grainy Dijon mustard
3	cloves garlic, minced
1–4 Tbsp (15–60 mL)	balsamic vinegar
¼ cup (60 mL)	red wine vinegar
to taste	salt and freshly ground black pepper
½ cup (125 mL)	extra virgin olive oil
1 Tbsp (15 mL)	minced fresh thyme
1 tsp (5 mL)	minced fresh rosemary

Whisk together the mustard, garlic, vinegars, salt and pepper. Slowly add the oil, whisking to emulsify. Stir in the herbs. Store in the refrigerator for up to a week.

VARIATIONS   Olive and Anchovy Vinaigrette Add minced oil-cured olives and puréed anchovies to taste.
Tomato Vinaigrette For a tomato-based vinaigrette, whisk in tomato dice. Fresh tomatoes make a volatile dressing with a brief life span, so use it within a day or two.

TIP   Fresh is the only useful type of rosemary for a cook, as dried becomes musty and overly pungent. Gardening cooks should find a sturdy potted rosemary to see them through the winter. It likes heat and light, and thrives as a groundcover in hospitable climates like the Mediterranean and Southern California. A plant flourishing on a windowsill can take you on a culinary magic carpet ride, transporting you to sunny Provençal hillsides, the air heavy with the scent of summer and rosemary.

LOW-FAT RECIPES

Pear & Chive Vinaigrette

makes about 1 cup (250 mL) ⓥ

DEE HOBSBAWN-SMITH FROM *SKINNY FEASTS*

1	pear, peeled and sliced
⅓ cup (80 mL)	sherry vinegar or Japanese rice vinegar
2 Tbsp (30 mL)	liquid honey
2 Tbsp (30 mL)	minced fresh chives
1 Tbsp (15 mL)	puréed fresh ginger
1–6 tsp (5–30 mL)	wasabi
¼ cup (60 mL)	canola oil
to taste	salt and hot chili flakes

In a nonstick pan, cook the pear slices over high heat in a small amount of the canola oil. Allow the slices to brown, turning as needed. Put through a food mill or purée in a food processor. Add the remaining ingredients and whisk well.

TIP Wasabi, or Japanese horseradish, comes in a powdered green form or a paste in groceries that carry Japanese goods. I prefer the powder; its delicate green tint is a wonderfully ironic counterpoint to its fierce character. Reconstitute by adding water to the powder and stirring until smooth. Make and use small amounts: this is a culinary powder keg! In a pinch, substitute horseradish.

Maple Lime Dressing

makes about 1 cup (250 mL)

SHAUNA RATNER AND FRANCES JOHNSON FROM *EATING LIGHT, EATING RIGHT*

2	limes, juice of
¼ cup (60 mL)	maple syrup
¼ cup (60 mL)	Dijon mustard
¼ cup (60 mL)	olive oil
½ tsp (2 mL)	salt
dash	ground black pepper

In a small jar, combine all ingredients. Shake well.

Raspberry Salad Dressing

makes ½ cup (125 mL)

LIZ PEARSON AND MAIRLYN SMITH FROM
THE ULTIMATE HEALTHY EATING PLAN

5 Tbsp (75 mL)	raspberry cocktail concentrate, thawed
1 Tbsp + 1 tsp (20 mL)	canola oil
1	shallot, minced
¼ tsp (1 mL)	Dijon mustard
¼ tsp (1 mL)	paprika
¼ tsp (1 mL)	freshly cracked pepper

Whisk together all the ingredients. Can be stored for up to 1 week in the refrigerator.

Low-Fat Ranch Dressing

makes 1 cup (250 mL)

NORENE GILLETZ FROM *THE FOOD PROCESSOR BIBLE*

½ cup (125 mL)	light mayonnaise
¼ cup (60 mL)	fat-free yogurt
¼ cup (60 mL)	skim milk
2 tsp (10 mL)	white vinegar
1 tsp (5 mL)	Dijon mustard
1 tsp (5 mL)	liquid honey
½ tsp (2 mL)	dried basil

Using a food processor fitted with a steel blade, process all ingredients until blended, about 10 seconds. Keeps for 5 or 6 days in the refrigerator.

LOW-FAT RECIPES

Peasant Vegetable Vinaigrette

makes about 1½ cups (375 mL) 🌿

DEE HOBSBAWN-SMITH FROM *SKINNY FEASTS*

2	onions, peeled and quartered
1	whole head garlic, unpeeled
2 sprigs	fresh rosemary
1–2 Tbsp (15–30 mL)	extra virgin olive oil
2–3 Tbsp (30–45 mL)	liquid honey
1 Tbsp (15 mL)	grainy mustard
2–4 Tbsp (30–60 mL)	balsamic or red wine vinegar
2	green onions, minced
	water or stock for thinning
to taste	salt and freshly ground black pepper

Set the oven at 450°F (230°C) and put the onions into a small roasting pan or ovenproof baking dish in a single layer. (Too deep a layer and they will steam and take much longer.) Add the garlic, intact and still in its "paper," then add 1 sprig of rosemary and drizzle the olive oil over all.

Slide the pan into the hot oven, and roast the onions until brown on top and tender inside, about 45 to 60 minutes, depending on their size.

Once the onions are tender, transfer them to a food processor, adding the roasted garlic by squeezing out the pulp of each clove. Process into a smooth purée, then add the remaining rosemary leaves and all the remaining ingredients. Process to the texture you like—smooth or chunky. Thin to taste with water or stock, adding salt and pepper at the end to balance the flavors.

VARIATIONS Roasted Tomato and Basil Vinaigrette Substitute 2 to
3 roasted Roma tomatoes for the onions and ¼ cup
(60 mL) minced fresh basil for the rosemary.
Roasted Parsnip and Sage Dressing Substitute 1 medium roasted parsnip for the onions and ¼ cup (60 mL)
minced fresh sage for the rosemary.
Roasted Carrot and Dill Dressing Substitute 1 to
2 roasted carrots for the onions and 2 Tbsp (30 mL)
minced fresh dill for the rosemary. Add ½ tsp (2 mL)
cracked caraway seed if desired.
Roasted Sweet Potato and Tarragon Dressing Replace
the onions with half a roasted yam or sweet potato.
Replace the rosemary with 2 Tbsp (30 mL) minced
fresh tarragon.
Roasted Beet and Dill Dressing Use 1 to 2 roasted
golden or purple beets with 2 Tbsp (30 mL) minced
fresh dill in place of the onions and rosemary. Roast
the beets whole and in their skins, wrapping them
in aluminum foil. Slip the skins off like an old jacket
when the beets are cooked.

Yummy Yogurt
Salad Dressing

makes about 1¼ cups (310 mL)

NORENE GILLETZ FROM *THE FOOD PROCESSOR BIBLE*

½	small onion
2 Tbsp (30 mL)	fresh parsley (or 2 tsp/10 mL dried parsley)
1 cup (250 mL)	yogurt (fat free or regular)
2–3 Tbsp (30–45 mL)	canola oil
1 Tbsp (15 mL)	white vinegar
½ tsp (2 mL)	salt
dash	freshly ground black pepper
¼ tsp (1 mL)	each dried oregano, dried basil and garlic powder
pinch	dried tarragon

Using a food processor fitted with a steel blade, process onion with parsley until minced. Add remaining ingredients and process about 10 seconds longer. Chill for 1 hour before serving to blend flavors. Keeps about 10 days in a tightly covered container in the refrigerator.

VARIATION   Omit dried tarragon and dried basil. Add 2 Tbsp (30 mL) fresh basil and/or dill. Add 2 Tbsp (30 mL) chili sauce or ketchup, if desired.

Quark Tarragon Dressing

makes 1½ cups (375 mL)

DEE HOBSBAWN-SMITH FROM *SKINNY FEASTS*

1 cup (250 mL)	quark
1	shallot, minced
2	cloves garlic, puréed
2 Tbsp (30 mL)	minced fresh tarragon
1 Tbsp (15 mL)	minced fresh chives
⅛ tsp (0.5 mL)	cracked fennel seeds
½	lemon, juice and zest of
2 Tbsp (30 mL)	tarragon-infused vinegar (see page 113)
2 Tbsp (30 mL)	canola oil
to taste	salt and hot chili flakes

Combine all ingredients and whisk together, adding cool water or buttermilk to thin if desired.

TIP Quark is a European fresh cheese, very tart and soft. It is possible to substitute ricotta or goat cheese.

Greenhouse Dip

makes about 1½ cups (375 mL)

DEE HOBSBAWN-SMITH FROM *SKINNY FEASTS*

½ bunch	green onions (green part only)
¼ bunch	cilantro, stems discarded
¼ bunch	fresh parsley, stems discarded
2	cloves garlic
1½ tsp (7.5 mL)	grated fresh ginger
½ cup (125 mL)	mayonnaise
½ cup (125 mL)	sour cream
1½ tsp (7.5 mL)	lemon juice
1½ tsp (7.5 mL)	light soy sauce
1 tsp (5 mL)	Worcestershire sauce
1 tsp (5 mL)	ground cumin
1 tsp (5 mL)	ground coriander
¼–½ tsp (1–2 mL)	hot chili paste
¼ tsp (1 mL)	sesame oil

Cut the green onions into 2-inch (5 cm) lengths, reserving the white part for use in another dish. In a food processor, finely purée the green onions, cilantro, parsley, garlic and ginger. Add the remaining ingredients and process until well blended. Taste and balance with additional lemon juice, soy sauce or hot chili paste as your palate dictates.

House Dressing

makes ½ cup (125 mL) 🌱

LIZ PEARSON AND MAIRLYN SMITH FROM *THE ULTIMATE HEALTHY EATING PLAN*

¼ cup (60 mL)	balsamic vinegar
1 Tbsp + 1 tsp (20 mL)	extra virgin olive oil
1 Tbsp (15 mL)	water
2 tsp (10 mL)	grainy Dijon mustard
2 tsp (10 mL)	honey
1	clove garlic, crushed

Whisk together all the ingredients. Can be stored in the refrigerator for up to 1 week.

Creamy Maple Yogurt Dressing

makes about 1⅓ cups (330 mL) 🌿

LIZ PEARSON AND MAIRLYN SMITH FROM *THE ULTIMATE HEALTHY EATING PLAN*

6 Tbsp (90 mL)	low-fat mayonnaise
6 Tbsp (90 mL)	low-fat plain yogurt
6 Tbsp (90 mL)	cider vinegar
3 Tbsp (45 mL)	maple syrup

Whisk together all the ingredients.

Creamy Lemon Yogurt

makes about 1¾ cups (435 mL)

SHAUNA RATNER AND FRANCES JOHNSON FROM *EATING LIGHT, EATING RIGHT*

1 cup (250 mL)	low-fat plain yogurt
½ cup (125 mL)	fat-free mayonnaise
2 Tbsp (30 mL)	lemon juice
2 Tbsp (30 mL)	sugar
½ tsp (2 mL)	salt
½ tsp (2 mL)	ground black pepper

Whisk all the ingredients together and mix well.

Don's Fiery Avocado Dressing

makes about 1 cup (250 mL)

DEE HOBSBAWN-SMITH FROM *THE QUICK GOURMET*

½	avocado, mashed
¼ cup (60 mL)	yogurt or sour cream
1	lime, juice and zest of
1	morita chili, rehydrated and puréed
½ tsp (2 mL)	curry paste
¼ tsp (1 mL)	cumin seed
to taste	salt

Combine all the ingredients, thinning with additional yogurt or sour cream if necessary.

TIP Dried chilies and chili powder are readily found in specialty food stores or health food stores. Chilies, both fresh and dried, have spawned their own culture, cookbooks, magazine and hip lingo. There are increasing numbers of varieties available and, to add to the confusion for the uninitiated, some fresh chilies change their names when they are dried. The jalapeño becomes the morita or chipotle when it is smoked and dried. The ancho, however, remains the ancho in both fresh and dried forms. Chimayo chili powder is pure ground New Mexico chili from the Chimayo area south of Santa Fe, grown high in the Sangre de Cristo Mountains. Substitute regular chili powder if you cannot find it.

2

Miso-Gari Vinaigrette

makes about 1 cup (250 mL)

DEE HOBSBAWN-SMITH FROM *SKINNY FEASTS*

1½ tsp–1 Tbsp (7.5–15 mL)	white miso
½	lemon, juice and zest of
½ cup (125 mL)	Japanese rice vinegar
2 Tbsp (30 mL)	soy sauce
2 Tbsp (30 mL)	melted honey
1 Tbsp (15 mL)	sesame oil
1 Tbsp (15 mL)	minced pickled ginger
1 Tbsp (15 mL)	minced cilantro
2	green onions, finely minced
to taste	salt and hot chili flakes

Combine all ingredients and refrigerate until needed. Best within 3 days of being made.

TIP Miso is one of those amazing ingredients that can insinuate itself into any number of dishes. It is a high-protein fermented paste made from soy beans that may be flavored with rice or barley. Flavors and colors vary, so the best bet is to buy several varieties and taste them to see which you prefer. Generally, the lighter the color, the lighter the flavor. Miso is found in good Asian supermarkets and in health food stores, and is always stored in the refrigerator. A spoonful of miso dissolved in hot water makes miso soup, one of the world's most restorative instant soups.

Ponzu Vinaigrette

makes about 1¼ cups (310 mL)

DEE HOBSBAWN-SMITH FROM *SKINNY FEASTS*

½ cup (125 mL)	rice vinegar
½ cup (125 mL)	fresh lemon juice
¼ cup (60 mL)	dark soy sauce
to taste	hot chili paste
2 Tbsp (30 mL)	minced chives or green onions
2 Tbsp (30 mL)	minced cilantro
1 Tbsp (15 mL)	minced fresh ginger
2 tsp (10 mL)	sesame oil

Whisk together all the ingredients.

Asian Salad Dressing

makes about 1 cup (250 mL) 🌿

NORENE GILLETZ FROM *THE FOOD PROCESSOR BIBLE*

2	cloves garlic
½ cup (125 mL)	rice vinegar
¼ cup (60 mL)	canola oil
¼ cup (60 mL)	soy sauce
3–4 Tbsp (45–60 mL)	honey (or to taste)
2 Tbsp (30 mL)	toasted sesame oil
2 Tbsp (30 mL)	toasted sesame seeds

Using a food processor fitted with a steel blade, drop the garlic through the feed tube while machine is running and process until minced. Add remaining ingredients and process until blended, about 10 to 15 seconds. Store in a jar in the refrigerator for up to 1 month. Shake well before using.

Buttermilk Herb Dressing

makes about 1 cup (250 mL) 🌿

DEE HOBSBAWN-SMITH FROM *THE QUICK GOURMET*

½ cup (125 mL)	sour cream or yogurt, drained
½ cup (125 mL)	buttermilk
½	lemon or lime, juice and zest of
½ bunch	spinach, minced or puréed
1 Tbsp (15 mL) EACH	minced fresh thyme, oregano, basil, parsley, mint and rosemary
1½ tsp (7.5 mL)	grated fresh ginger
2	cloves garlic, minced
⅛ tsp (0.5 mL)	cracked fennel seed
to taste	salt and hot chili flakes

Combine all the ingredients by hand or in a food processor and allow to mellow for several hours before using. Keeps well in the refrigerator for up to a week.

VARIATIONS For a spicier kick to this lush dressing, substitute watercress for the spinach. For the puckery taste of green apple, use sorrel in place of the suggested herbs.

Yukon Gold Potato Salad with Olives & Mustard Rosemary Dressing

makes about 8 cups (2 L) ❧

DEE HOBSBAWN-SMITH FROM *THE QUICK GOURMET*

2 lb (1 kg)	Yukon Gold potatoes, diced
2	red bell peppers
1 cup (250 mL)	kalamata olives, pitted and chopped
¼ cup (60 mL)	capers, drained
1 bunch	green onions, minced
2	stalks celery, minced
½ cup (125 mL)	Onions in Orange Juice (see facing page)
¼ cup (60 mL)	grainy Dijon mustard
2–3	sprigs fresh rosemary, finely minced
4	cloves garlic, minced
¼ cup (60 mL)	melted honey
1	lemon, zest only
¼ cup (60 mL)	white wine vinegar
¼ cup (60 mL)	extra virgin olive oil
to taste	salt and freshly ground black pepper
¼ cup (60 mL)	minced fresh parsley
2 Tbsp (30 mL)	minced fresh thyme

Put the diced potatoes into a heavy pan and add cold water to a depth of 1 inch (2.5 cm). Cook the potatoes until tender. While they are cooking, roast the peppers over an open flame until the entire surface is blackened. Transfer the blackened peppers to a plastic bag to steam for 10 minutes, then remove the blackened skin and the seeds. Slice the peppers into strips 2 inches (5 cm) long and ¼ inch (0.5 cm) wide. Place in a bowl

with the olives, capers, green onions, celery and
Onions in Orange Juice (see below).

Make the dressing by whisking together the mustard, rosemary, garlic, honey, lemon zest, vinegar and olive oil. While the potatoes are still warm, toss them with the roasted pepper and vegetable mixture, then add the dressing. Mix well. Taste and season with salt and pepper, then stir in the parsley and thyme. Serve warm or cold.

Onions in Orange Juice

makes about 2 cups (500 mL)

½ lb (250 g)	sweet onions, finely sliced
1	orange, juice and zest of
1½ tsp (7.5 mL)	honey or white sugar
1½ tsp (7.5 mL)	minced fresh thyme
to taste	salt and hot chili flakes

Put the onion slices into a colander or sieve and pour boiling water over them. This makes the onions less strong-tasting and more amenable to pickling. Drain well. Combine the remaining ingredients and toss with the warm onion slices. Cover and chill.

Smoky Bacon Vinaigrette

makes about 1½ cups (375 mL)

MARY ELLEN ELLIOT FROM *EAT TO THE BEAT* (EDITED BY LISA SLATER)

6 slices	thick-cut bacon, coarsely chopped
1 cup (250 mL)	grapeseed oil
½ cup (125 mL)	red wine vinegar
splash	balsamic vinegar
2 Tbsp (30 mL)	chopped fresh herbs (parsley, dill, thyme etc.)
to taste	salt and pepper

Fry the bacon until crisp. Remove to a paper towel and set aside one-third of the bacon fat from the pan. Place the bacon in a stainless steel bowl with the reserved bacon fat. Add the grapeseed oil, red wine vinegar, balsamic vinegar, chopped herbs, salt and pepper. Whisk together.

NOODLE & POTATO SALADS

145

Moroccan Spicy
Potato Salad Dressing

makes about 1 cup (250 mL) ✻ ERIC AKIS FROM *EVERYONE CAN COOK*

2	lemons, juice of
4	cloves garlic, crushed
6	green onions, finely chopped
6 Tbsp (90 mL)	chopped fresh mint
1 Tbsp (15 mL)	ground cumin
1 Tbsp (15 mL)	paprika
½ tsp (2 mL)	cayenne pepper
2 tsp (10 mL)	sugar
½ cup (125 mL)	olive oil
to taste	salt and freshly cracked black pepper

Combine all the ingredients, except the salt and pepper, in a large bowl, mixing well. Season with salt and pepper.

VARIATIONS A nice addition to this salad dressing is 1 cup (250 mL) chopped green or black olives. If fresh mint is not available you can substitute 3 Tbsp (45 mL) dried mint.

Thai Herb Vinaigrette

makes about 1½ cups (375 mL) 🌿

GLENYS MORGAN FROM *GIRLS WHO DISH! SECONDS ANYONE?*

6 cloves	garlic, finely minced
¼ cup (60 mL)	brown sugar
2	limes, zest and juice of
¼ cup (60 mL)	nam pla (Thai fish sauce)
1 Tbsp (15 mL)	sambal oelek (Indonesian hot sauce)
1 cup (250 mL)	chopped cilantro, mint, basil or a combination

Whisk together the garlic, brown sugar, lime juice and zest, nam pla, and sambal oelek, as well as the herbs if using immediately. If preparing the dressing ahead of time, the herbs should be added just before serving to avoid darkening.

NOODLE & POTATO SALADS

Cilantro Pesto Dressing

makes about 1½ cups (375 mL) 🌿

MARGARET CHISHOLM FROM *GIRLS WHO DISH! SECONDS ANYONE?*

1 cup (250 mL)	fresh cilantro leaves
¾ cup (185 mL)	fresh spinach
½	clove garlic, chopped
1½ Tbsp (22.5 mL)	olive oil
1 Tbsp (15 mL)	lime juice
6 Tbsp (90 mL)	Parmesan cheese

Combine the cilantro, spinach, garlic, olive oil and lime juice in a food processor. Process until a smooth paste forms, scraping down the sides of the bowl occasionally. Place the mixture in a large bowl and stir in the Parmesan cheese.

Black Bean & Garlic Ginger Dressing

makes about 1⅓ cups (330 mL) ❦

CAREN McSHERRY FROM *GIRLS WHO DISH! SECONDS ANYONE?*

1	large shallot, finely minced
¼ cup (60 mL)	soy sauce
2 Tbsp (30 mL)	rice vinegar
1 Tbsp (15 mL)	chopped fermented black beans
1 Tbsp (15 mL)	minced fresh ginger
2 Tbsp (30 mL)	sesame oil, preferably Kadoya brand
2	cloves garlic, minced
1 Tbsp (15 mL)	chili paste (optional)
¾ cup (185 mL)	grapeseed oil
to taste	salt and pepper

Prepare the dressing by whisking together the shallot, soy sauce, rice vinegar, black beans, ginger, sesame oil, garlic and chili paste. Slowly pour the oil into the bowl, whisking the entire time. Taste for seasoning.

Thai Peanut Sesame Noodle Dressing

makes about 1¾ cups (435 mL) 🌿

NATHAN HYAM FROM *NEW THAI CUISINE*

6 Tbsp (90 mL)	vegetable oil
¼ cup (60 mL)	sesame oil
2	cloves garlic, crushed
2 Tbsp (30 mL)	peanut butter
2	small green chilies, seeded and very finely chopped
6 Tbsp (90 mL)	toasted sesame seeds
½ cup (125 mL)	soy sauce
¼ cup (60 mL)	lime juice
to taste	salt and black pepper

Mix the oils with the garlic and peanut butter until smooth. Add the chilies, sesame seeds, soy sauce and lime juice, and mix well. Season with salt and pepper.

Thai Noodle
Salad Dressing

makes about ⅔ cup (160 mL) 🌿

SUE DONALDSON FROM *FOODS THAT DON'T BITE BACK*

3 Tbsp (45 mL)	lime juice
2 Tbsp (30 mL)	toasted (dark) sesame oil
1½ Tbsp (22.5 mL)	grated fresh ginger
3	cloves garlic, minced
1½ Tbsp (22.5 mL)	tamari
1 Tbsp (15 mL)	rice vinegar
1 Tbsp (15 mL)	sugar
1–1½ tsp (5–7.5 mL)	chili paste

Whisk together all the ingredients.

Red Chili Dressing

makes about 1⅓ cups (330 mL) ◙ JOHN GARRETT FROM *HORIZONS*

½ cup (125 mL)	rice wine vinegar
½ cup (125 mL)	brown chicken stock
1 Tbsp (15 mL)	lime juice
1	shallot, peeled and minced
2 tsp (10 mL)	peeled and minced fresh ginger
3 Tbsp (45 mL)	chili garlic sauce
1 tsp (5 mL)	soy sauce
1 tsp (5 mL)	sesame oil

Whisk all the ingredients together. Refrigerate until ready to use. This vinaigrette will keep in the refrigerator for 1 day.

TIP Brown chicken stock is made from roasted chicken bones and has a deeper, more complex flavor than regular stock. However, regular chicken stock can be used.

Shanghai Noodle Dressing

makes 1¼ cups (310 mL)

SUSAN MENDELSON AND JOEY CRUZ FROM *THE LAZY GOURMET*

2 Tbsp (30 mL)	peanut butter (unsweetened, smooth)
1½ tsp (7.5 mL)	freshly grated ginger
1 tsp (5 mL)	sambal oelek (Indonesian hot sauce)
5 Tbsp (75 mL)	liquid honey
3 Tbsp (45 mL)	rice wine vinegar
3 Tbsp (45 mL)	soy sauce
2 Tbsp (30 mL)	sesame oil
5 Tbsp (75 mL)	vegetable oil

Thoroughly combine all the ingredients in a blender.

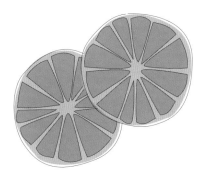

Orange Cardamom Dressing

makes about 1⅓ cups (330 mL) 🌿

SUE DONALDSON FROM FOODS *THAT DON'T BITE BACK*

1 cup (250 mL)	orange juice
2 Tbsp (30 mL)	olive oil
2 Tbsp (30 mL)	maple syrup
2 tsp (10 mL)	ground coriander
1 tsp (5 mL)	ground cardamom

Whisk together all the ingredients.

(Adapted from the Moosewood Collective's *Moosewood Restaurant Low-Fat Favorites.*)

Maple Mustard Dressing

makes 1 cup (250 mL) 🌿

SUE DONALDSON FROM *FOODS THAT DON'T BITE BACK*

½ cup (125 mL) olive oil
3 Tbsp (45 mL) Dijon mustard
3 Tbsp (45 mL) apple cider vinegar
2 Tbsp (30 mL) maple syrup
1½ tsp (7.5 mL) salt

Whisk together all the ingredients.

Contributors

Eric Akis   *Everyone Can Cook*

Eric Akis is food writer for the Victoria *Times Colonist* and a food colum-
nist for several Canadian newspapers. He is the author of the Canadian
bestselling *Everyone Can Cook* series including *Everyone Can Cook,
Everyone Can Cook Seafood, Everyone Can Cook Appetizers, Everyone Can
Cook Midweek Meals* and *Everyone Can Cook for Celebrations*.

Dan Atkinson   *Salmon House on the Hill Cookbook*

One of Vancouver's most imaginative chefs, Dan has worked at the
Salmon House on the Hill restaurant since the early 1990s. His primary
influences are the fresh ingredients found throughout the Pacific
Northwest, from the bounty of the ocean to the fresh produce of the
Fraser Valley.

Karen Barnaby   *Girls Who Dish! Seconds Anyone?*
Inspirations

Karen has been executive chef at the Fish House in Stanley Park since
1995. She's the award-winning author of *Pacific Passions Cookbook,
Screamingly Good Food* and *The Passionate Cook* and a coauthor of *The
Girls Who Dish!, The Girls Who Dish! Seconds Anyone?* and *Inspirations* as
well as the *David Wood Food Book* and *David Wood Dessert Book*. More
recently she edited *Halibut: The Cookbook* and *Shellfish: The Cookbook*.

Cinda Chavich   *Dishing*

Cinda has spent the past 25 years as a journalist writing for Canadian
newspapers and magazines. She has traveled the world, poking into kitchens wherever she goes, but her roots are in Western Canada and her passion is regional cuisine and the stories of those who share that passion.
She is the author of the bestselling *Wild West Cookbook, The Best Pressure*

Many of the titles mentioned in this section are available through Whitecap Books.

Cooker Recipes, High Plains: The Joy of Alberta Cuisine, The Girl Can't Cook and *The Guy Can't Cook,* and has received a Cuisine Canada Award.

Margaret Chisholm   *Girls Who Dish! Seconds Anyone?*

Margaret has worked in catering, taught budding chefs for five years at the Dubrulle Culinary Institute in Vancouver and been executive chef at Culinary Capers Catering. As a full-service caterer, she can whip up a picnic for two or a dinner for thousands.

Deb Connors   *Girls Who Dish! Seconds Anyone?*

Deb helped open Vancouver's famous Joe Fortes Restaurant, and worked as a sous chef at the Salmon House on the Hill and as head chef at Horizons restaurant. She also helped plan and launch Aqua Riva. Her kitchen philosophy is "Give people what they want, but do it your own way."

Sue Donaldson   *Foods That Don't Bite Back*

Sue Donaldson is the Kingston, Ontario, author of a vegan recipe collection. She has also written a historical mystery novel for young adults entitled *Thread of Deceit*, published under the pseudonym Susan Cliffe.

Anne Donnelly   *Eat to the Beat*

For the past 26 years, Anne has been executive chef of Arcadian Court at the Hudson's Bay Company in Toronto. She began her European-based hotel career in Ireland, followed by six years in Switzerland, then a move to Toronto to join the Bay's York Street location. Anne's favorite cuisine is sushi and her choice of three guests at her dinner table would be her grandmother, Julia Child and John Wayne.

Mary Ellen Elliot   *Eat to the Beat*

Mary Ellen is grandmother and inspiration to Jason Rosso—the former executive chef of Niagara's Peller Estates and now director of operations of Toronto's Distillery Restaurants.

John Garrett   *Horizons*

John Garrett has given Burnaby, BC, the ultimate West Coast dining experience with his bold, imaginative menu. Leading the helm of Horizon's kitchen, John has won numerous awards and has published the *Horizons* cookbook.

Norene Gilletz   *The Food Processor Bible*

Norene Gilletz is the leading author of kosher cookbooks in Canada. Her books include *The Food Processor Bible, MealLeaniYumm!, Healthy Helpings, Second Helpings Please* and *Norene's Healthy Kitchen*. A culinary consultant, food writer and cooking teacher, she can usually be found within close range of a kitchen (not always her own!). Norene is a Certified Culinary Professional with the International Association of Culinary Professionals, and a member of Cuisine Canada and the Women's Culinary Network of Toronto. Norene's culinary expertise has earned her a place in *Canadian Who's Who*.

dee Hobsbawn-Smith   *Dishing*
The Quick Gourmet
Skinny Feasts

A poet, author, educator and food writer for the *Calgary Herald*, dee Hobsbawn-Smith grows flowers, cultivates ideas and sows the seeds of content from her home office in Calgary. When she grows up, she hopes to make enough money to support a year in south-central France or northern Spain to write the Next Great Canadian Poetry Collection. Dee's work appears in Canadian magazines and in her books *Skinny Feasts, The Quick Gourmet* and *The Curious Cook at Home*. She has two sons.

Nathan Hyam   *New Thai Cuisine*

(The new recipes written by Nathan Hyam for this collection are Quick Honey Mustard Dressing, Basic Coleslaw Dressing, Western ("French") Dressing, Blue Cheese Dressing, Creamy Spinach Salad Dressing, Thousand Island Dressing and Thai Creamy Caesar Dressing.)

After travels to Thailand, many Thai cooking courses and mentoring by acclaimed Thai chefs, New York City–born Nathan Hyam has come to be known as "the Thai guy." His first book was *New Thai Cuisine*. He is the editor of this collection.

Bill Jones   *Chef's Salad*

Bill Jones is a chef, author and food consultant based on Vancouver Island. He is the author of six cookbooks and the editor of *Salmon: The Cookbook*, and winner of a 2003 Gourmand World Cookbook award. Bill is the proprietor of Magnetic North Cuisine and operates a culinary tourism venture from its home base, Deerholme Farm (www.magnorth.bc.ca).

Ellen Kelly   *Dishing*

Ellen Kelly has worked as a food and cookbook writer, chef, restaurant consultant, caterer and cooking instructor at various times during the many years she has spent as a culinary professional. At present, she devotes her time and energy to the *City Palate* magazine, writing about food and selling advertising in the industry she loves and supports.

Dana McCauley   *Pantry Raid*

Dana McCauley is the former food editor of *Homemakers* and *Style at Home* magazines and an accomplished cookbook author whose books include *Last Dinner on the Titanic* (cowritten with Rick Archbold), *Noodles Express*, *Pantry Raid* and *Homemaker's Menu of the Month Cookbook*. She blogs for Homemakers.com, contributes to various magazines and has appeared on over a hundred TV shows in the US and Canada. Visit her blog at www.homemakers.com/blog/danasblog/.

Mary Mackay   *Girls Who Dish! Seconds Anyone?*
Inspirations

Mary Mackay began cultivating her sense of the importance of food from a very early age. As a graduate of the Dubrulle Culinary School, a member of Les Dames d'Escoffier and head baker and co-owner of Terra Breads, she is always seeking to create fun and unusual ways to play with food.

Caren McSherry *More Than Salt and Pepper*
Girls Who Dish! Seconds Anyone?

With her worldwide culinary education, successful cooking school (Canada's longest running), unique wholesale foods business and exuberant personality, Caren McSherry is one of the best-known names in the Canadian culinary industry. She has contributed to *Girls Who Dish! Seconds Anyone?* and authored *More than Salt and Pepper: 25 Years of Spicing Up the Kitchen.*

Susan Mendelson and Joey Cruz *The Lazy Gourmet*

An entrepreneur, celebrity and cookbook author, Susan started a catering business called The Lazy Gourmet and has won numerous awards, including the Consumers' Choice Award for Best Caterer, and been recognized as one of the top 100 Business Women in Canada by *Chatelaine.* Susan has published several books, including *Mama Never Cooked Like This, Let Me in the Kitchen* and *Nuts about Chocolate.* Joey Cruz has been the executive chef at The Lazy Gourmet.

Olaf Mertens *Cooking from the Hip*

A cofounder of Chefs of Canada Society, the Captain of Team Canada of the Epicurean World Master Chefs' Society and a designated Küchenmeister (Master Chef) having completed a degree at the Steigenberger Hotel School in Europe, Olaf is an exuberantly active member of his profession. He is the executive chef and co-owner of On The Curve Hot Stove & Wine Bar in Mississauga and author of *Olaf's Kitchen* and *Cooking from the Hip.*

Karen Miller *Dishing*

Karen loves the entertaining part of food. A lawyer for many years, she started catering with a friend.

Joan Monfaredi *Eat to the Beat*

Joan has been the executive chef at the Park Hyatt Hotel in Toronto since 1999.

Glenys Morgan   *Girls Who Dish! Seconds Anyone?*

Glenys has opened her own cooking school and stores and worked as a consultant. She has inspired budding cooks at the Dubrulle Culinary School and been inducted into Les Dames d'Escoffier.

Gail Norton   *Dishing*
              Double Dishing

Always drawn to the social aspects of cooking and eating with friends and family, Gail Norton opened a cookbook store, The Cookbook Co., with her mother. The Cookbook Co. Cooks is now Calgary's premier cooking school. Gail is publisher of Calgary's *City Palate* and a founding member of Slow Food Calgary, and has cowritten *Cooks in My Kitchen: Tales and Recipes from a Cooking School* with Diane Thuna.

Anna and Michael Olson   *Inn on the Twenty*

Anna is the very popular host of Food Network Canada's *Sugar* and *Fresh with Anna Olson*. She is the author of *Sugar, Another Cup of Sugar, Fresh with Anna Olson* and *In the Kitchen with Anna*. Michael is chef-professor at the Niagara Culinary Institute, Niagara College.

Liz Pearson and Mairlyn Smith   *The Ultimate Healthy Eating Plan*

With her emphasis on fun food in moderation, Liz is one of Canada's most high-profile nutrition experts. She runs the Pearson Institute of Nutrition, which converts nutrition research into a format accessible to consumers. Mairlyn is a multitalented home economist, teacher and actor who loves to add a dash of comedy to her cooking. Their most recent book is *Ultimate Foods for Ultimate Health*.

Shauna Ratner and Frances Johnson   *Eating Light, Eating Right*

Shauna works as a dietitian and has a passion for food and healthy eating. Her goal is to help others make healthier choices while still experiencing the pleasure of flavorful food. Frances, as an award-winning dietitian, understands the importance of enjoying nutritious and flavorful food as part of maintaining a healthy lifestyle. Their first book was *Eating Light and Loving It!*

Shelley Robinson   *Double Dishing*

Shelley's modern, eclectic cuisine has been the delight of several Calgary-area restaurants (including her own—Lake Louise's Baker Creek Bistro), countless catering clients, cooking classes and appreciative family and friends.

Kathleen Sloan-McIntosh   *A Year in Niagara*

Kathleen has been writing about food and drink for three decades. Her work has appeared in many major magazines and newspapers in Canada and abroad. She is the author of *Rustic Italian Cooking* and *The Global Grill* and coauthor of the Cuisine Canada Silver Award–winning *The Sticks & Stones Cookbook*. She has also coauthored *New Celtic Cooking*, with her husband, Ted McIntosh. Her book *A Year in Niagara: the People and Food of Wine Country* won a Silver Cuisine Canada Book Award.

Lesley Stowe   *Girls Who Dish! Seconds Anyone?*
                Inspirations

Trained in Paris, Lesley has worked as a caterer and food retailer. She has also taught cooking at her store in Vancouver, as well as in Calgary and as far away as Italy, at Umberto's Villa Delia in Tuscany.

Jennifer Warren   *Vegetarian Comfort Food*

Jennifer Warren grew up in her parents' restaurant, where she frequently got underfoot in the kitchen and learned how to cook along the way. She writes, edits and comes up with great new vegetarian recipes in Montreal.

Janet Webb   *Double Dishing*
              Dishing

Janet has worked as wine sommelier and opened one of Alberta's first privately owned wine boutiques. After studying at the Beringer Cooking School in California, she returned to Calgary to share her knowledge of pairing food and wine.

Judy Wood   *Dishing*
            Double Dishing

Judy received her *Grand Diplôme* from the famed L'École de Cuisine La
Varenne in Paris. She has worked at the Four Seasons Hotel in Calgary, as
a pastry chef at the David Wood Food Shop in Toronto and as head chef
at Buchanan's in Calgary. She joined Sunterra Food group in 1990 and in
1998 became the founder and executive chef of Savoury Café & Catering.
She received the Woman of Vision award in Calgary in 1999. She is now
co-owner and executive chef of Mise en Place—a "meal assembly studio
kitchen" in Calgary.

Pairing Suggestions

1 Delicate Mild-Flavored Greens

Asian Salad Dressing 138
Avocado Green Goddess Dressing 81
Balsamic Vinaigrette 120
Basic Vinaigrette 12
Basil Balsamic Vinaigrette 15
Black Bean & Garlic Ginger Dressing 149
Blue Cheese Dressing 68
Buttermilk Herb Dressing 139
Cal-Ital Dressing 56
Caesar Dressing 99
Caesar Vinaigrette 96
Caramelized Apple Vinaigrette 119
Champagne Vinaigrette 16
Cilantro Ginger Vinaigrette 40
Cilantro Pesto Dressing 148
Citrus Vanilla Vinaigrette 18
Citrus Vinaigrette 17
Classic Caesar Dressing 95
Cranberry Pecan Dressing 29
Cranberry Tamari Dressing 24
Creamy Caesar Dressing 98
Creamy Dill Salad Dressing 74
Creamy Dressing #1 78
Creamy Dressing #2 79
Creamy Garlic Dressing 76
Creamy Gorgonzola Dressing 70
Creamy Green Curry Dressing 82
Creamy Herb Dressing 67
Creamy Indian Curry Dressing 83
Creamy Lemon Yogurt 133
Creamy Maple Yogurt Dressing 132
Creamy Spinach Salad Dressing 73
Don's Fiery Avocado Dressing 134
Fresh Tomato Dressing 46
Gorgonzola Dressing 69
Grapefruit Vinaigrette 23
Green Goddess Salad Dressing 80
Greenhouse Dip 130
Hazelnut Vinaigrette 114

Honey Balsamic Vinaigrette 32
Honey Caper Vinaigrette 33
House Dressing 131
Italian Salad Dressing 52
Lemon Ginger Vinaigrette 37
Lemon Honey Dressing 20
Light & Delicious Caesar Dressing 100
Light of Heart Tarragon Dressing 109
Light Tarragon Vinaigrette 112
Low-Fat Ranch Dressing 125
Mango Chutney Cream 84
Mango Chutney Walnut Vinaigrette 51
Maple Lime Dressing 123

2 Sturdy Robust-Flavored Greens

Anchovy Vinaigrette 45
Asian Salad Dressing 138
Asian Sesame Vinaigrette 42
Balsamic Vinaigrette 120
Basic Coleslaw Dressing 60
Basic Vinaigrette 12
Maple Mustard Dressing 155
Maple Syrup Vinaigrette 55
Maple Thyme Vinaigrette 116
Marty's Garlic Cheese Dressing 77
Mayo Magic (Basic Safe Mayo) 66
Minted Caesar Dressing 101
Miso-Gari Vinaigrette 136
Modern Caesar Dressing 97
Mustard Honey Pesto Vinaigrette 50
Orange Ginger Sesame Dressing 38
Orange Peanut Ginger Dressing 85
Pear & Chive Vinaigrette 122
Peasant Vegetable Vinaigrette 126
Pickled Ginger & Avocado Dressing 86
Pickled Ginger Vinaigrette 35
Ponzu Vinaigrette 137
Port Cherry Dressing 30
Prairie Sage Vinaigrette 113

3 Starches

Index

Page numbers in italics indicate that the item is used in a variation rather than in a recipe proper.

T

tangerine 22
tapenade 43
tarragon 13, 14, 70, 109, 112, 119, *127*, 129
   vinegar 70
Thai-style dressing and vinaigrette 36, 39,
      82, 87, 88, 150, 151
Thousand Island Dressing 75, 89
thyme *12*, 27, 32, 47, 57, 67, 106, 108, *111*, 116,
      117, 119, 120, 139, 142, 145
   lemon thyme 114
tomato 46, *121*, *127*

V

vanilla 18, 19

W

walnuts 51
   walnut oil 31, 57
wasabi, about 122
wine 108

Y

yogurt 78, 79, 80, 82, 100, 128, 132, 133, 134

Z

Zinfandel Vinaigrette 108